Fisherwomen on the Kerala coast

Women, Work and Development, 8

Fisherwomen on the Kerala coast

Demographic and socio-economic impact of a fisheries development project

Leela Gulati

Published with the financial support of the
United Nations Fund for Population Activities
(UNFPA)

International Labour Office   Geneva

Gulati, L.
Fisherwomen on the Kerala coast: Demographic and socio-economic impact of a fisheries development project
Geneva, International Labour Office, 1984. Women, Work and Development, No. 8

/Report/ on the /Fertility/ implications, /Social implication/s and /Economic implication/s for /Women/ of a /Fishery development/ project in Kerala, /India/. 14.04
ISBN 92-2-103626-X
ISSN 0253-2042

ILO Cataloguing in Publication Data

Printed in Germany   BKL

PREFACE

Over 30 years ago the Norwegian government, in collaboration with the Indian government, began what came to be known as the Indo-Norwegian Fisheries Development Project. Mechanised boats and improved gear were introduced to modernise fishing and use of ice and freezing were introduced to improve the preservation of the fish caught in several villages in Kerala in an effort to increase productivity and income levels in what were then very poor villages. Also introduced were improved health facilities and sanitation.

This was a development project which was successful in meeting its objectives. Income rose dramatically — partly due to the chance discovery of prawn beds in an area beyond the range of traditional boats. And, mortality rates fell precipitously.

The present study focuses on the economic and demographic impacts brought about by the major changes introduced by this development project. The author investigates these effects in three villages which have had different experiences.

What distinguishes this study from earlier analyses of this major development project is its focus on women. This is in contrast to the core aspects of the project on modernising fishing and fish processing which did not show concern for women *per se* probably due to the fact that women do not go out fishing. Neglected at the time were the facts (1) that women traditionally participate in preservation, distribution and marketing of fish and (2) that any major technological change would have major spin-off effects in terms of income opportunities for women.

The author adopted a case study approach, amassing over the years detailed information about the lives of 30 women and their households in the three study villages. In this monograph, detailed biographical sketches are provided for ten of these women. These biographies make compelling reading, vividly portraying the trials and tribulations of these women and how their lives have changed over time. They illustrate how useful such a micro-approach can be.

To these in-depth case study data, the author added macro survey data, government statistical information and data taken from church records. This combination of quantitative and qualitative, macro and micro information helps the author to present a complete picture of the changing situation of women and families in the three study villages in the context of extensive socio-economic-demographic change over the past 30 years.

The author's evaluation of the development experience in the three study villages indicates that even though women were excluded from the core programme aimed at modernising fishing and fish preservation, they were still able to take advantage of the opportunities created by the new situation. Women's participation in income-generating and wage-earning activities increased as they began to work for wages as food processors (especially prawn peeling) and to earn money by repairing the nylon nets. This demonstrates how women are able to take advantage of work opportunities when they are made available.

The author points out that women should also have been given relevant training to help them develop their skills and to help them form effective co-operatives. Another clear policy implication she rightly draws is that there is hardly a development project which does not have an implicit women's dimension (whether planned or not) and she rightly contends that if in the design and implementation of the programme, care had been taken to assign fisherwomen a part in the modern processing, freezing and trading of fish, their present participation would be more widespread, on a larger scale and less marginal and exploitative. As it is, their work tends to be seasonal (along with the prawn catch) for low wages in unhygienic and unhealthy conditions — even if there are improvements over previous generations in the type of work and amount of income earned.

Her conclusion is that in the context of the technological and other changes introduced by the Indo-Norwegian Fisheries Development Project, one of the most dramatic changes has been with respect to family size which is linked to both lower infant mortality, widespread availability and use of hospital facilities and fertility control. A clear lesson from this study is that economic development in conjunction with the provision of health and family planning facilities do matter as regards fertility rates and family planning acceptance and that it is possible to achieve reductions in both mortality and fertility.

Richard Anker
Christine Oppong

ACKNOWLEDGEMENTS

I would like to express my gratitude to Mme Béguin and Gerry Rodgers of the ILO for their overall support and encouragement during my work on this project. I am also grateful to Richard Anker and Christine Oppong for their help throughout including, in particular, their assistance in editing and preparing the manuscript for publication. I am also very grateful to Father Puthenkulam for his guidance and help during the field work, and to the Centre for Development Studies, Trivandrum for providing full supporting services throughout my work. Finally I would like to express my gratitude to the Indian Council of Social Science for funding the exploratory work which led to the present study.

CONTENTS

PREFACE   v

INTRODUCTION   1

I   IMPACT OF A FISHERIES DEVELOPMENT
     PROJECT IN KERALA   5

     Importance of fisheries   5
     Indo-Norwegian Project   6
     Choice of Project   6
     Objectives of the Project   6
     The Project site   7
     Technological impact and change   7
     The mix of species   10
     Preoccupation with prawn   11
     Seasonality of operations   12
     Growth of freezing activity   12

II   DEMOGRAPHIC PROFILE OF KERALA STATE   15

     Population density   15
     Literacy level   15
     Population growth rates   16
     Sectoral changes in birth and death rates   18
     Regional and religious differences   19
     Sex ratio   20
     Female age at marriage   21
     Marital fertility and family planning   22
     Characteristics of sterilisations   23
     Religious factor in sterilisations   25
     Concluding observations   25

III PROFILE OF PROJECT VILLAGES   27

     A. The Project Area   27

         Population of the karas   29
         Fishing population   29
         Religious composition of the fishing households   31
         Sex ratio   31
         Average household size   32
         Housing conditions   33
         Literacy ratios   34
         Work participation and occupational distribution   36
         Civil condition   37
         Occupational distribution   37

B. Sakthikulangara Village   40

    The public boat jetty   41
    Electricity connection   42
    Drinking water   42
    Toilet facilities   43
    Financial institutions and sources of credit   43
    Educational facilities   44
    Medical facilities   44
    The church in Sakthikulangara   45
    The church records   45
    Births and deaths   45
    Choice of institution   47
    Age at marriage   47

C. Neendakara Village   48

    Economic integration of the two villages   49
    Points of difference   49
    Economic and social infrastructure   50
    Births and deaths   50
    Age at marriage   52
    Looking ahead   53

D. Puthenthura Village   53

    The Foundation Hospital   54
    Family planning   54
    The Araya fishermen   55
    The Araya Seva Samithi   55
    The west side settlement   56
    The east side settlement   56
    The fish landing site   57
    Age at marriage   58
    Pregnancies per married woman   59
    Acceptance of family planning   59

Summary of observations   60

    Technological change   60
    Economic change   61
    Demographic changes   62
    Overall changes   63

IV PROFILES OF WOMEN   65

    Sakthikulangara

        Case Study – A   MAGGIE – The headload fish vendor   65

        Case Study – B   PHILOMENA – The non-working wife   74

        Case Study – C   MARY – The prawn peeler   80

        Case Study – D   LILLY FRANCIS – The boat owner's wife   87

        Case Study – E   GORATTI – A deck-hand's wife   93

    Neendakara

        Case Study – A   KADALAMMA – The boat manager   100

        Case Study – B   BEATRICE – The prawn dealer   108

    Puthenthura

        Case Study – A   RAMANI – The net maker   118

        Case Study – B   SARLA – The chit fund operator   126

        Case Study – C   PANKAJAKSHI – A retired home-maker   134

V WOMEN'S CHANGING ROLES   141

    Involvement in work of the previous generation   141
    Work involvement of the present generation   142
    Involvement in work of the younger generation   143
    Work and change in lifestyles   143
    Literacy level   144
    Importance of marriage   144
    Age at marriage   145
    Arranged marriage   145
    Spread of dowry   146
    Dowry in recent years   147
    Dowry among the Arayas   147
    Composition of the dowry   147
    Mobilising the dowry and modes of payment   147
    Use of dowry money   148
    Family size   148
    Type of care at childbirth   150
    Child mortality   151
    Feeding and birth interval   151
    Family planning status   152

SOME GENERAL OBSERVATIONS AND SUGGESTIONS   153

LIST OF TABLES

Table I   Distribution of case studies by principal male occupation   3

Table I.1   Operation of traditional and mechanised crafts in the Project area   8
Table I.2   Annual sea fish landings in Neendakara (in '000 tonnes)   9
Table I.3   Percentage composition of catches of mechanised boats at
                 Neendakara in the total mechanised fishery of Kerala
                 during 1973–1976   10
Table I.4   Trend in prawn production by mechanised boats at Neendakara
                 during 1973–1979   11
Table I.5   Ice plants, freezing plants and capacity in Kerala, 1953, 1963,
                 1968, 1976   13

Table II.1   Population and population density, Kerala and India, 1901–81   15
Table II.2   Literacy rates, Kerala and India, 1901–81   16
Table II.3   Intercensal rates of population growth in Kerala and India, 1901–81   17
Table II.4   Birth and death rates in Kerala and India, 1931–1979   17
Table II.5   Birth and death rates in rural and urban Kerala, 1966–1979   18
Table II.6   Birth rates in Kerala State by region and religion, 1977   19
Table II.7   Accessibility and utilisation of medical care, and mortality rates in
                 the natural regions of Kerala State   20
Table II.8   Sex ratio in Kerala and India, 1901–81   20
Table II.9   Sex ratio (females per thousand males) among the fishing population
                 in the districts of Kerala State, 1971   21
Table II.10   Mean female age at marriage in Kerala and India,
                 1901–10 to 1961–70   22
Table II.11   Percentage of couples protected by various family planning
                 methods in Kerala State   23
Table II.12   Male, female, and total sterilisations in Kerala State,
                 1960–61 to 1979–80   23
Table II.13   Percentage of sterilised persons according to age and sex in Kerala,
                 1967–68, 1970–71, 1973–74   24
Table II.14   Percentage distribution of sterilised persons according to number of
                 children living in Kerala, 1967-68, 1970–71, 1973–74   25
Table II.15   Percentage distribution of sterilisations by religion, 1961,
                 1970–71 to 1973–74   25

Table III.1   Population, sex ratio and literacy rates in Sakthikulangara
                 and Neendakara, 1951, 1961, 1971   29
Table III.2   Fishing population in Project villages, 1953, 1959, 1963, 1978   30
Table III.3   Religious composition of fishing households in
                 Project villages, 1978   31
Table III.4   Sex ratio in Project villages, 1953, 1959, 1963, 1978   32
Table III.5   Average size of fishing households in Project villages,
                 1953, 1959, 1963, 1978   32

Table III.6   Percentage distribution of fishing households by size in Project
               villages, 1953, 1978   33
Table III.7   Percentage distribution of fishing households in Project
               villages by type of dwelling, 1953, 1978   34
Table III.8   Literacy rates (total, male and female) in Project karas and
               rural Quilon, 1951, 1961, 1971   35
Table III.9   Literacy rates among fishermen of the Project karas, 1959, 1963   35
Table III.10   Percentage distribution of fishermen of Project villages by
               sex and educational attainment, 1978   36
Table III.11   Male and female work participation rates in Project
               villages, 1978   36
Table III.12   Percentage distribution of working women by civil condition, 1978   37
Table III.13   Percentage distribution of working fishermen in Project villages
               by nature of work, 1978   38
Table III.14   Ownership distribution of mechanised boats in Project
               villages, 1978   39
Table III.15   Percentage distribution of working women from fishing households
               in Project villages by nature of work, 1978   39

Sakthikulangara Village   40

Table III.16   Birth and death rates in Sakthikulangara Parish, 1950–79   45
Table III.17   Distribution of births in Sakthikulangara by place of delivery
               and type of institution, 1950–79   46
Table III.18   Mean age at first marriage in Sakthikulangara Parish, 1901–79   48

Neendakara Village   48

Table III.19   Birth and death rates in Neendakara Parish, 1950–79   51
Table III.20   Distribution of births in Neendakara by place of delivery and
               type of institution, 1950–79   52
Table III.21   Mean age at first marriage in Neendakara Parish, 1901–79   53

Puthenthura Village   53

Table III.22   Mean female age at marriage in Project villages, 1931–80   58
Table III.23   Average number of live pregnancies per married woman in
               Project villages   59
Table III.24   Acceptance of family planning in Project villages   60

INTRODUCTION

Some three decades ago (1953), a project was taken up in a block of three traditional fishing villages in the State of Kerala, with a view to introducing modern technologies of fishing and fish preservation. Mechanised boats and improved gear were introduced to modernise fishing and the use of ice and freezing were introduced to improve the preservation of the fish caught. While the primary emphasis was on increased productivity in fishing and fish preservation, the Project also envisaged providing better health services and sanitation in and around the three villages. The purpose of this study was to discover and document how the resulting changes in the technology of fishing and fish preservation in Kerala communities have affected women of fishing households, not only in general economic terms, but also specifically in terms of demographic behaviour.

Clearly, the Project, as it was conceived and designed, was mainly geared towards men in the community. Since women did not go out fishing, it was assumed that change in the technology of fishing was of no direct concern to women. However, women did participate to some extent in the preservation, distribution and marketing of the fish caught under traditional methods. But the Project did not show concern for women as such in the measures envisaged for the improvement of fish preservation, distribution and marketing. The only change to be directed explicitly towards women of the Project area was the introduction of better sanitation and medical health facilities.

The basic underlying assumption of the Project was that if men of the fishing households could be helped to improve their economic position, their womenfolk would automatically stand to gain. Very often this assumption is justified on the grounds that either women in these households are not doing anything economically productive, or even if they are involved in economically productive work, it is not of much consequence or concern. These assumptions, to say the least, are quite arguable.

Questions such as the following have seldom been raised: how do women adjust to major technological changes in the work of their menfolk; or what measures should be taken to draw women into the new situation created by technological changes? Indeed, women themselves have such a low estimation of their work and its return that they themselves are least concerned about their involvement (or the lack of it) in work, present or prospective. Yet when circumstances so change as to deprive women of what little work they are able to do, it can adversely affect certain households. Actually the decline in figures of women's work participation in India since the turn of the century clearly shows that technological advance has tended to take work away from women. In spite of the clear evidence in this regard, still very little attention is paid to this aspect in most schemes and projects envisaging the introduction of new technology. Is it any wonder that the Project meant principally to modernise fishing and fish preservation showed little concern for the women of the households directly affected? Would it take work away from these women or create some new work opportunities for them? This is a question that the Project did not concern itself with. The purpose of this study is to raise this question in retrospect. Having raised this question and attempted answers, the study goes on to ask what, if any, changes have

1

come about in the fertility behaviour of those women also have lived through a major technological change for almost a generation.

Although the three original fishing villages chosen for the aforesaid modernisation Project form a geographically compact block, the fishing folk of these villages are drawn from two quite distinct religious groups, Latin Catholic and Araya Hindu. The acceptance of technological change was distinctly different between these groups, although there can be genuine debate about the role of the religious factor in this difference in acceptance.

With this background, the present study concerns itself with the following major questions:

1) As a result of changes that have occurred in the technology of fishing, what change has occurred in the work status of women?

2) Is this change different for the two religious groups?

3) As a result of changes in women's work participation, has there been any change in the status and roles of women?

4) What change has occurred in the fertility behaviour of women from these fishing households?

5) Are there any differences or disparities that exist with regard to fertility behaviour between the two religious groups?

In order to answer the questions posed above, the present study relies considerably on case studies. At the same time, use has been made of information available on the basis of surveys and censuses from these villages. In addition, new surveys were undertaken as part of the present study where it was found necessary to have supplementary information or to check information available from other surveys. It was our feeling that while a sample survey would enable generalisations at the macro level, it is only through case studies that one gained insight into the real processes at work at the micro level.

Both approaches have their drawbacks. One has always to strike a compromise. In this study, however, it was decided to rely principally on case studies for two reasons. First, existing information on the occupational status of women in fishing households and on their status and roles within the household available from various surveys and censuses of fishing households was very scanty. A comprehensive survey of households to elicit all relevant information was beyond the scope of this study. Second, but not less important, it was felt that the impact of change which this study was focusing on could better be studied through intensive case studies.

Of the various methods of conducting case studies, we have used the autobiographical method. Each principal respondent tells her own story, as reconstructed over a period of intensive contact with her, her household, her relations, friends, neighbours, employers, etc.

Choice of case studies

To start with, fishing households were chosen on the basis of a random stratified sample; ten households were chosen from each of three villages. These households were chosen from lists of households obtained from the parish church records in the two Christian villages, and from the records of Araya Samithi (the caste association of Araya fishermen) in the Hindu village. The households were grouped according to the occupation/sub-occupation of the principal male workers in the household. Thus, men engaged in fishing were subdivided according to whether they were owners of mechanised boats or traditional craft, or whether they worked as crew for mechanised boats or traditional craft. For each of the 30 chosen households, information was collected on family genealogy, including names, relationships of all relatives, age, place of birth, education, dowry, occupation, number of children born alive or dead, and family planning status. On average it was possible to collect information for each family on 26 related couples covering three generations. Thus, information was collected on 784 married couples in all. Though the preparation of genealogies was very time consuming, it was found rewarding because it enabled us to fill in the gaps found in the information available at the macro level from other sources based on surveys and/or censuses covering the villages under study.

Only ten households were chosen out of the above 30 for biographical sketches. The distribution of these ten households over the occupational categories is given in Table I.

Table I   Distribution of case studies by principal male occupation

Occupation/ sub-occupation	Distribution of 30 case study households	Distribution of 10 case study households with reported biographical sketches
Craft owners		
(a) Traditional	8	4
(b) Mechanised	5	2
Crew		
(a) Traditional	6	1
(b) Mechanised	8	1
Others	3	2
Total	30	10

Source: Author's study

3

The decision to present only ten autobiographies, rather than all 30 which were collected, was made for a number of reasons. First, because of similarity there would have been a considerable amount of repetition. Also, a few of the households were not fully cooperative. That not every one is equally willing to put up with personal questions week after week for a period of 12 to 18 months is something that social scientists engaged in ethnographical work would readily appreciate. As a result, no doubt, a certain amount of arbitrariness can be said to have crept into the choice of the biographical sketches presented here. It must be added, however, that the choice of households for biographical study covers all major categories of working women in addition to a few non-working women. The biographical sketches presented in this report have to be viewed, nonetheless, in the background of the macro-level information that has been presented in this report.

The organisation of the report

Three chapters give the background information (i) on the Project that sought to introduce technological change in fishing and fish preservation and its aftermath, (ii) on the demographic profile of Kerala State as a whole, and (iii) on the profiles of the three fishing villages. In outlining the macro-level picture, full use is made of the information from available surveys and censuses. Where necessary, use is also made of the survey information that was collected as part of the present study. The village profiles and the ten biographies can be said to constitute the core of this study. In the concluding chapter, an attempt is made to draw broad inferences from the biographical sketches in light of the background of the macro-level picture presented in the first three chapters. Changes in women's roles, given the technological, economic and demographic change the studied families and their environment have undergone for more than three decades, are the focus.

CHAPTER I

IMPACT OF A FISHERIES DEVELOPMENT
PROJECT IN KERALA

Kerala is one of the leading maritime states in India. It has a long coastline of 590 kilometres and a network of rivers, lakes and water areas which make it ideal for fishing. The waters of Kerala also are by far the richest in the country. The intermixing of the nutrient-laden waters from the 41 west-flowing rivers with the seawater all along the coast is the reason for such a long stretch of fishable area. Kerala has a fishable area as large as that of the land surface of the state. The coastline is dotted with many protected bays, estuaries and natural harbours which provide excellent facilities for the launching and landing of fishing crafts. As a result, the coastline is spread with 249 fishing villages, amounting to almost a village every 2 1/4 kilometres along the coastline.

The fishing population of Kerala as a whole is about 770,000, forming 159,000 households. Thus one out of every 30 fishing households in the state is that of a fisherman. If we were to make a distinction between those who fish in the deep sea and those who fish in the inland waters, we have 114,000 as marine fishing households and 45,000 inland fishing households, and there are about 160,000 active fishermen. The industry provides employment to another 350,000 persons.

Fishing families in Kerala belong to three major religious groups, namely, Hindus, Christians and Muslims. Though in the total population these religious groups are distributed in the ratio of 60 : 20 : 20, in the fishing population they are more or less evenly distributed, their ratio being 40 : 35 : 25. In other words, the fishing households form a major group particularly among the Christian and the Muslim households.

Importance of fisheries

Fishing occupies an important place in the economy of Kerala, as it is an important source of food and protein, it is a major avenue of employment, and in recent years, it has become a major export industry. Kerala's population is essentially a fish-eating population; the level of fish consumption in Kerala is four times the national average. Until very recently fish was a relatively cheap source of protein. In the early part of the 1970s, fish consumption stood at 15 kg per capita per annum. This figure has, however, been declining, but the fact remains that even in the humblest of households there is at least one meal with fish everyday. Eggs, milk or meat rarely enter the diet. Fish remains an integral part of the food.

The people engaged in fisheries come under three distinct groups: (i) those employed in the actual catching of fish, (ii) those engaged in the processing, and (iii) those engaged in the making of fishing equipment such as craft and gear. There is some overlap between these groups but when one usually talks of fishermen, one is referring to people falling in the first group.

5

With the high population pressure and high unemployment in the state, fisheries are a great source of economic diversification.

Traditionally there existed some export of dried fish and prawn powder from Kerala to the South East Asian countries. This activity was, however, marginal. The major preoccupation was to meet the domestic consumption requirements of fish for the population of the state and the border districts of the neighbouring state. In recent years, however, export of prawns has become a major national economic activity and Kerala's share in it is very significant, being close to 50 per cent. The total quantity of prawns exported went up twelve times between 1963 and 1977. In terms of value, the expansion was 40 times. Today, marine products rank as the third largest commodity export of the country with prawns accounting for over 90% of the value of such exports.

Indo-Norwegian Project

The Indo-Norwegian Project was one of the earliest external aid projects agreed upon after India became independent in August 1947. It also happened to be the first Scandinavian effort in India, reflecting the enthusiasm and motivation of the ruling Labour Party in Norway to extend concrete help to less developed countries, in an area where not only could the Norwegians offer technical know-how on the basis of their own long experience, but also where benefits were most likely to reach the lower income groups of the countries being assisted.

Choice of Project

The Norwegians were anxious, and quite understandably so, that whatever aid they provided should have a clear focus in terms of economic activity, beneficiaries, and location, and that it should be concentrated, so that its effects could be visible within a reasonable period of time.

At the same time, since Kerala was a major maritime state of India with a sizable part of its population depending on fishing for its livelihood, it was felt that the start could be made in Kerala. Also around that time, Kerala State itself was seriously considering the introduction of some amount of mechanisation in fishing.

Objectives of the Project

The primary objectives of this particular Project were stated to be:
(a) to bring about an increase in the income of the fishermen;
(b) to introduce an efficient distribution of fresh fish and thereby improve the fish products;
(c) to improve the health and sanitary conditions of the fishing population; and
(d) to raise the standard of living of the community in the Project area in general.

The fulfilment of the above objectives was to be promoted by the Project, principally through mechanisation of fishing. More concretely, the Project envisaged the following:

6

(a) mechanisation of existing crafts;
(b) introduction of suitable new mechanised boats;
(c) introduction of ice and improved freezing techniques for the preservation of fish; and
(d) use of insulated vans in fish disposal.

Thus, the Project aimed at introducing simultaneously fundamental changes in boat and gear technology as well as in processing and marketing. With the introduction of these changes it was hoped that the Project would not only help in raising the living standards of fishermen, but bring about a local social and economic transformation as well.

The Project site

With a view to applying aid effort in a concentrated form, three contiguous fishing villages in the district of Quilon were selected for the purpose. The three villages, covering an area of 25 square kilometres, are located on National Highway 47 going from Cape Comorin to Salem (see map 1, Project Area). The villages are located some 9 kilometres north of the city of Quilon. The three villages belong to two different Panchayats. While the larger one belongs to the Sakthikulangara Panchayat, the smaller two belong to the Neendakara Panchayat. The highway bridge constructed on the Ashtamudi Lake connects Sakthikulangara with the other two to its north. All three villages are also well connected by various link roads with the interior regions and other districts of the state. In terms of social composition, Sakthikulangara and Neendakara are predominantly Latin Catholic and Puthenthura is a Hindu fishing village.

Technological impact and change

It is nearly 27 years since the Project was launched in these villages and seventeen years since the Project was completed. During this period, a number of major changes have occurred in the economies of these villages, though not each village has been affected in the same way by these changes.

The foremost change has been in the technology of fishing in that, while in 1953 no mechanised boat was operated by the fishermen in these villages, the number currently operated by local fishermen is 419. On the other hand, there has been a steep decline during the same period in the number of traditional crafts operated by the fishermen of these villages. Table I.1 brings out the shift from traditional crafts to mechanised boats.

Table I.1   Operation of traditional and mechanised crafts in the Project area

	Year	Mechanised boats	Traditional crafts	
			Thanguvallom (large plank-built craft)	Kochuvallom (small plank-built craft)
1	1953	–	197	280
2	1959	63	123	260
3	1963	87	93	135
4	1976	144	35	48
5	1980	419	40	147

Note: *Thanguvallom,* the larger of the two types of craft used in this area, is 40 feet long and carries a crew of 9 to 11 men. It operates a local purse-seine net called *thanguvala.* The vessel currently costs around Rs. 15,000.
Kochuvallom, which is narrower and about 30 feet long, carries a crew of 4 to 6 men. It costs between Rs. 5,000 and Rs. 6,500.

Sources: 1953 – Bog (1954).
1959 – Indo-Norwegian Project Standing Committee (1960), p. 29.
1963 – Indo-Norwegian Project Standing Committee (1960) and Asari and Menon (1969), p. 34.
1976 – Kerala State, Development Department, (1976), Part I, p. 5.
1980 – Information collected specially for this study.

The extent of change-over to mechanised fishing is reflected even more forcefully in the statistics of fish catch. The quantity of fish caught in the Project area in 1953 stood around 2,000 tonnes, all of which was the contribution of traditional craft. In 1968, the total catch was estimated at 12,800 tonnes. But, as can be seen from Table I.2, the contribution of the traditional crafts had declined to a mere 6.3 per cent of the total catch. In fact, the catch of the traditional craft had declined in absolute terms. Between 1968 and 1979, the catch contributed by mechanised craft had registered a further substantial increase, even though during this period there were very wide fluctuations in annual catch, a matter which is a subject of considerable concern currently. It is quite clear that as far as the Project area is concerned, mechanised fishing has almost completely eclipsed the role of the traditional crafts. An important reason for the catch increasing so greatly in the Project area is that a very large number of boats from other districts ply here during certain months, particularly from June to September, considered the peak fishing season for prawns. It is estimated that during this season, not less than 2,000 mechanised boats operate in this area and unload their catch in the jetties located in the Neendakara Fishing Harbour.

Table I.2   Annual sea fish landings in Neendakara (in '000 tonnes)

Year	Total catch	Catch by mecha-nised crafts	Percentage of Col (3) to Col (2)
(1)	(2)	(3)	(4)
1953	2.00	–	–
1959	2.08	0.26	12.5
1960	2.79	0.71	25.4
1961	2.63	0.88	33.5
1962	1.30	0.64	49.2
1968	12.80	12.00	93.7
1970		26.704	
1971		31.493	
1972		23.622	
1973		66.064	
1974		77.748	
1975		1,51.095	
1976		29.836	
1977		45.828	
1978		89.892	
1979		56.016	
1980		84.556	

Sources: 1. Asari and Menon (1969).
2. Central Marine Fisheries Research Institute (1981).

The Neendakara Fishing Harbour is an all-weather landing centre, and it is particularly popular because of the occurrence of prawns in this area, especially during the months of June to August; both are responsible for the overcrowding at this jetty. The catch from this area, particularly during the three months of July, August and September, has accounted for one-half to three-fourths of the total catch of mechanised boats recorded at the 23 landing centres in Kerala State (see Table I.3).

Table I.3 Percentage composition of catches of mechanised boats at Neendakara in the total mechanised fishery of Kerala during 1973–1979

Year	Total catch of mechanised boats in Kerala (tonnes)	Total catch of mechanised boats in Neendakara (tonnes)	Percentage of Neendakara catch to the all Kerala catch
1973	93 659	66 064	70.54
1974	101 412	77 748	76.67
1975	180 717	151 095	83.89
1976	58 717	29 836	50.89
1977	107 424	45 828	42.66
1978	117 356	89 892	76.60
1979	95 191	56 016	58.85

Source: George (1980b).

Neendakara Harbour is perhaps the biggest landing centre in the country with the greatest number of boats engaged in prawn trawling. Though the trawling operations are carried out almost throughout the year, a characteristic feature noticed in the area is that peak fishing activities are restricted to a brief period of three months which account for almost three-fourths of the annual catch. Hundreds of boats, not only from other parts of the state, but also from outside the state, assemble here and temporarily camp until the season is over. Only during the rest of the year are the local boats left to themselves to go out to fish for whatever is available in the sea. Of course, the traditional fishermen are always there but their operations have declined over the years in this area.

The mix of species

Before 1953, the fish caught in the Neendakara area were sardine, butter fish and mackerel. On the introduction of mechanised boats, fishermen in the area started fishing for sharks and seer fish which lay in waters beyond the reach of the traditional craft. During the latter part of the 1960s however, the composition of the catch switched considerably in favour of the prawns. Today fishing for prawns dominates the whole catch effort in the area.

Preoccupation with prawn

It would not be an exaggeration to say that fishing in the Neendakara area has come to stand for fishing for prawns. No doubt, some quantity of prawns were caught in this region prior to the introduction of mechanised fishing, but this was collected mainly in the backwaters and paddy fields by traditional canoes and it comprised a very small portion of the total catch. Also the type of prawn caught then not only had very little export demand but also was not one of the sought-after species domestically. Thus, there were occasions when there was an excess catch of prawns, a good part of which had to be left to rot to be used as fertiliser for coconut trees. A small quantity of backwater prawn was exported in the form of pulp or as dried fish to countries such as Burma and Sri Lanka. It was sometime during the early 1960s when one of the mechanised vessels "discovered" extensive grounds some 10 to 15 kilometres off the coast for catching prawn. This coincided with the opening up of the markets abroad, first in the USA and subsequently in Japan. Prawn exports from the Neendakara area have seldom had to look back since then. The external demand for prawns has been large and growing. The Neendakara area owes the expansion in its fishing activity almost entirely to this particular factor.

Table I.4   Trend in prawn production by mechanised boats at
Neendakara during 1973–1980

Year	Total catch (tonnes)	Prawn catch (tonnes)	Percentage of prawns in total catch
1973	66,064	45,477	68.8
1974	77,748	27,764	35.7
1975	1,51,095	56,750	37.6
1976	29,836	14,993	50.2
1977	45,828	24,121	52.6
1978	89,892	33,143	36.8
1979	56,016	14,582	26.0
1980	84,556	36,559	43.2

Source: George (1980b).

Fishing for prawns has come to dominate the scene in Neendakara. Although, as can be seen from Table I.4, the ratio of prawns to total annual landings has fluctuated rather widely from year to year, the overriding fact remains that the recent fishing activity revolves around the catching of prawns. All other species are only by-products of the fishing activity in the Neendakara area. Notwithstanding the fact that recently the ratio of prawns to total catch had dropped to almost 25 per cent — and notwithstanding a decline in absolute quantity of catch — the Neendakara

11

area remains the most important centre in the country for prawn landings and is likely to remain so for years to come.

Prawn fishing in the area is carried out mostly in mechanised boats of up to 14 metres in length, operating two to four sea prawn trawls at depths of up to 40 metres. These vessels go out on daily cruises, starting from the base early in the morning and returning in the evening.

Seasonality of operations

In theory, the trawling operations are carried out throughout the year, but a characteristic feature noticed in the area is that the peak fishing activities are concentrated in a short period of about three months during the south west monsoons, between June and September every year. Over 80% of the landings in the Neendakara area are accounted for by this period. This lends a far more pronounced seasonality to trawling than is true for traditional fishing. For the latter, the best three months account for about 40 per cent of the yearly catch. The next best three months account for another 35 per cent. The worst three months account for only 8 per cent of the catch in a year.

Growth of freezing activity

There was virtually no freezing activity connected with fishing before the mid-1950s in Kerala State. The prawns from inland waters were boiled in seawater or brine and dried or processed. The finished product was exported as prawn pulp, also called Burma pulp, Burma being the main export market. Prawn pulp was a low priced export article, and prawn fishing was not a very profitable activity for the fishermen to engage in. As for other species, excess catch on peak days was always salted and dried. That was the traditional method of processing fish. Of course, not all species could easily be dried and processed. At the same time, there used to be considerable waste through spoilage and delay in transportation of fish to centres of consumption, particularly when these were located away from the sea coast.

The use of ice for preserving fish had to be made popular and a climate of acceptance created. Once the use of ice was introduced, it also led to new methods of handling, processing and distribution. Today, ice is used extensively not only in the handling of prawns which are largely exported, but also in the preservation of other species. Even traditional fishermen and fisherwomen have taken to the use of ice. Among the consuming public also there is an increasing acceptance of fish kept in ice, and the prejudice that even the slightest use of ice impinges on the freshness and taste of fish is wearing out fast.

When keeping fish in ice was virtually unknown, the fish caught were unloaded and stored in heaps in the craft until it got back to the shore. This led to considerable spoilage of fish. Further spoilage occurred when the fresh fish was transported to hinterlands in open canoes or on cycles and lorries. Now mechanised vessels carry ice with them so that the catch can be iced immediately after it is taken out of the nets. As in the case of any fish, the persons buying prawns off the boats at the jetties see to it that they are iced forthwith. While prawns transported over long distances, as for example to Cochin port, are taken in refrigerated vans, other species are taken in trucks well stacked with ice. Table I.5 gives the figures for the growth in number of ice plants and freezing facilities in Kerala State over the period 1953 to 1976. In spite of phenomenal expansion, however, during the peak season there is a shortage of ice with the result that the price of ice fluctuates considerably in the course of a year. In fact, there is wide fluctuation from day to day, depending upon the catch on a particular day.

Table I.5   Ice plants, freezing plants and capacity in Kerala, 1953, 1963, 1968, 1976

Year	Ice plants			Freezing plants		
	No.	Production (tonnes)	Storage (tonnes)	No.	Freezing capacity (tonnes)	Frozen storage capacity (tonnes)
1953	–	–	–	–	–	–
1963	1	25	200	1	9	125
1968*	–	83	385	–	37	400
1976*	29	377	325	15	88	1,625

Sources: * 1. Asari and Menon (1969), p. 10.
            2. Kerala State, Development Department (1976), p. 11.

In summary, there is no doubt that as far as the Neendakara area is concerned, fishing has undergone a revolutionary change regard to the technology of fishing, the composition of catch and the technology of fish preservation. Also, since prawns comprise a major part of fish catch and since they are largely exported, it has had downstream linkages in the form of prawn processing, refrigeration and transportation that were unknown to this area before.

It is in the light of the above changes that we shall discuss the demographic and economic changes that have occurred in the lives of women in the three villages closest to the Neendakara Harbour in the last 25 years.

CHAPTER II

DEMOGRAPHIC PROFILE OF KERALA STATE

Kerala State has a number of unique demographic characteristics. While it has the highest population density in India, it also has the highest literacy rate (female as well as male), more women than men, the lowest mortality rates and the largest percentage of deliveries under institutional care in the country.

Population density

Though Kerala State occupies only 1.1 per cent of India's land area, it supports 3.9 per cent of its population. With 25.4 million people, Kerala's population density was 654 persons per square kilometre in 1981. This is four times higher than in 1901 (see Table II.1). These figures compare to a population density in 1981 of 221 for the country as a whole.

Table II.1   Population and population density, Kerala and India, 1901–1981

Year	Population in millions		Density per sq. km.	
	Kerala	India	Kerala	India
1901	6.89	238.39	165	73
1911	7.14	252.09	184	77
1921	7.80	251.32	201	77
1931	9.50	278.97	245	85
1941	11.03	318.66	284	97
1951	13.54	361.08	349	110
1961	16.90	439.23	435	134
1971	21.34	548.15	549	167
1981	25.40	683.81	654	221

Source: Government of India (1981).

Literacy level

In spite of its very high population density, the State of Kerala has been, throughout the current century, far ahead of the rest of the country in terms of the

15

percentage of total population which can read and write (Table II.2). What is just as significant is that over the years the gap between the sexes in literacy has been narrowed considerably. Thus, while for India as a whole the female literacy rate is only one-half the male literacy rate, for Kerala the female literacy rate is not only high in itself, being 64.5 per cent, but also quite close to the male literacy rate of 74 per cent. Moreover, rural-urban differentials in literacy levels are also quite narrow. For example, while the female literacy rate for the state as a whole was 53.9 per cent in 1971, the rate for the rural sector was 52.6 per cent. On the other hand, the female literacy rate was still rather low for scheduled castes and tribes, the social groups identified in the Constitution of India for certain preferential treatment in view of their relative social and economic backwardness. In 1971, the female literacy rate in Kerala was 33.3 per cent for scheduled castes and 18.5 per cent for scheduled tribes.

Table II.2   Literacy rates, Kerala and India, 1901–1981

Year	Kerala		India	
	Males	Females	Males	Females
1901	22.0	4.0	9.8	0.7
1911	26.0	5.0	10.6	1.1
1921	32.0	12.0	12.2	1.8
1931	37.0	14.0	15.6	2.9
1951	50.0	31.5	24.9	7.9
1961	54.2	38.4	34.4	12.9
1971	66.5	53.9	39.5	18.4
1981	74.0	64.5	46.7	24.9

Source: Government of India (1981).

Population growth rates

As can be seen from Table II.3, the population in Kerala State has been rising consistently from one census period to another at rates faster than those experienced by the country as a whole from 1901 to 1971. Only in the decade just concluded, i.e. 1971–81, has the population in Kerala grown at a lower rate than that experienced in the country as a whole.

16

Table II.3 Intercensal rates of population growth in Kerala and India, 1901–1981

Decade	Decennial variation Percentage rate of increase	
	Kerala	India
1901–10	+11.75	+ 5.75
1911–20	+ 9.16	− 0.31
1921–30	+21.85	+11.00
1931–40	+16.04	+14.22
1941–50	+22.28	+13.31
1951–60	+24.76	+21.51
1961–70	+26.29	+24.80
1971–80	+19.00	+24.75

Source: Government of India (1981).

A principal reason for higher rates of growth of population in Kerala, particularly from 1941 to 1971, was a substantial drop in mortality rates without a corresponding decline in fertility rates. This can be seen from Table II.4.

Table II.4 Birth and death rates in Kerala and India, 1931–1979

Period/ Year	Births rates (per thousand)		Death rates (per thousand)	
	Kerala	India	Kerala	India
1931–40	40.0	45.2	29.1	31.2
1941–50	39.8	39.9	22.3	27.4
1951–60	38.9	41.7	16.9	22.8
1968	33.2	39.0	10.0	16.8
1969	31.8	38.8	9.2	19.1
1970	31.6	36.8	9.2	15.7
1971	31.1	36.9	8.9	14.9
1972	31.2	36.6	9.2	16.9
1973	29.2	34.6	8.5	15.5
1974	26.8	34.5	7.8	14.5
1975	28.0	35.2	8.4	15.9
1976	27.8	34.4	8.1	15.0
1977	25.8	33.0	7.3	14.7
1978	25.2	33.3	7.0	14.2
1979	25.9	33.0	6.9	12.8

Source: Kerala State, Planning Board (1979).

While the death rate declined from 29.1 in 1931–40 to about 9 in 1970–71 (i.e. by approximately 20 points), the birth rate in the state declined from 40.0 to about 31 (i.e., by only approximately nine points) during the same period. During the decade of 1971–80, both the birth and death rates have registered further significant declines so that the birth and death rates were 25.9 and 6.9 per 1,000 in Kerala respectively in 1979, but the decline in birth rates was more than twice as steep, measured in terms of percentage points, than that in death rates. Additionally, there has been sizable net out-migration of people from Kerala to other states within India and other countries including the Gulf States during recent years, particularly in the latter part of the 1971–80 decade. According to a recent employment survey conducted in the state, as many as half a million workers lived outside the state during the first decade. Of these, 40 per cent went abroad.

Sectoral changes in birth and death rates

Data have been collected under a scheme of sample registration of births and deaths in the entire country since 1965–66. These data, which are believed to be

Table II.5   Birth and death rates in rural and urban Kerala, 1966–1979 (per thousand population)

Period/ Year	Birth rates		Death rates	
	Rural	Urban	Rural	Urban
1966	37.4	–	–	–
1967	36.3	–	–	–
1968	34.3	–	10.4	–
1969	33.3	–	–	–
1970	32.3	30.1	9.2	8.8
1971	32.9	29.6	9.8	8.4
1972	32.1	29.3	9.4	7.8
1973	29.9	28.4	8.6	7.2
1974	27.0	26.9	8.0	7.0
1975	27.8	27.3	8.5	7.8
1976	28.1	26.5	8.2	7.6
1977	26.1	24.1	7.4	6.8
1978	25.3	24.9	7.1	6.7
1979	26.1	24.8	7.0	–

Sources: 1. Kerala State, Bureau of Economics and Statistics (1977).
2. India, Registrar General, Sample Registration Bulletin (1974).
3. India, Registrar General, Sample Registration Bulletin (1980).

accurate in Kerala, show that birth and death rates in Kerala State declined not only in the urban sector, but also in the rural sector which accounts for some 80 per cent of the state's population. Table II.5 shows that while the rural birth rate fell from 34.3 per 1,000 population in 1968 to 26.1 in 1979, the decline in the death rate in the rural sector during the same period was from 10.4 to 7.0; as a result the natural rate of increase in the rural population declined during this period from 2.39 per cent to 1.91 per cent. From the point of view of the present study, the demographic trends in the rural sector are more relevant because the fishing population of the state is almost entirely non-urban.

Regional and religious differences

It is well known that the demographic parameters are different not only between religions but within a region among specific religious and socially disadvantaged groups. Hindus, Christians and Muslims are represented in the state's population in the ratio of 59 : 20 : 20. Among the Hindus, there exist caste divisions dating back over a thousand years. A few of the castes and tribes which are particularly disadvantaged have been identified in the Indian Constitution for preferential treatment in regard to certain matters of state policy. These groups are referred to as scheduled castes and tribes and comprise 10 per cent of Kerala's population. Fishing castes of Kerala State do not fall in the above category. They form part of what are referred to in the state as "backward castes" comprising over one-half of the Hindus in the state.

From Table II.6 it can be seen that birth rates differ greatly within the state between Hindus, Muslims and Christians and between highland and lowland and midland regions of the state.

Table II.6   Birth rates in Kerala State by region and religion, 1977 (per thousand)

Areas	Hindus	Muslims	Christians
Lowland	22.38	35.99	20.12
Midland	23.96	26.31	18.83
Highland	28.27	35.64	21.78

Source: Directorate of Economics and Statistics (1977).

We can see from Table II.7 that the number of beds per 100,000 population and the average area covered by medical centres varies considerably from region to region. This in turn seems to have affected the number of births attended with medical assistance, the death rate and the infant mortality rate in each region.

Not only is the percentage of births attended by medical personnel low, but the infant mortality is also high in the highlands. This in turn affects birth and death rates of the region.

On the whole, the percentage of births attended with medical assistance in Kerala is twice as high as that for the country as a whole.

19

Table II.7 Accessibility and utilisation of medical care, and mortality rates in the natural regions of Kerala State

	Lowland	Midland	Highland
No. of beds per 1,000 population (1970–71)	142.00	87.00	46.00
Average area (sq. kms) covered by medical centres (1970–71)	29.40	65.40	101.90
Percentage of deliveries using medical assistance (rural sector, 1977)	70.00	54.00	29.00
Death rate per 1,000 population (rural, 1977)	7.40	7.29	8.42
Infant deaths per 1,000 live births (rural, 1977)	44.90	46.60	71.40

Sources: 1. Krishnan (1976).
2. Directorate of Economics and Statistics (1977).

Sex ratio

The sex ratio in India is calculated according to the number of women for 1,000 males. From Table II.8, we can see that not only has the ratio of women to men in

Table II.8 Sex ratio in Kerala and India, 1901 to 1981

Year	Number of women per 1,000 men	
	Kerala	India
1901	1,004	972
1911	1,008	964
1921	1,011	956
1931	1,022	950
1941	1,027	945
1951	1,028	946
1961	1,022	941
1971	1,016	930
1981	1,034	935

Source: Government of India, Series 10, Kerala (1981).

Kerala been higher than for the country as a whole throughout the present century, but also the ratio has been always in favour of women in Kerala State unlike for the country as a whole.

However when one looks at the sex ratio among the fishing population, it cannot escape one's notice that there is a clear deficiency of women among fisherfolk. Table II.9 compares the sex ratio among fisherfolk in the various districts, where they are concentrated, with the corresponding sex ratio for the total rural population in each of these districts. It will be worthwhile noting that the rural sex ratio for the lowland region of Kerala is somewhat higher, being 1,027, as against 1,019 for the rural sector of the state taken as a whole. For purposes of comparing the sex ratio among fishermen, it is the rural ratio in the lowland region which should serve as a more appropriate yardstick, since practically all fishermen in the state live in the lowland region.

Table II.9   Sex ratio (females per thousand males) among the
fishing population in the districts of Kerala State, 1971

District	Fishing population	Rural population
(1)	(2)	(3)
Trivandrum	978.8	1,011
Quilon	976.7	1,002
Alleppey	969.2	1,029
Kottayam	952.7	976
Trichur	993.0	1,067
Kozhikode	964.6	990
Cannanore	988.1	1,018
Kerala State	974.7	1,019

Sources: Column (2): Kerala State, Department at Fisheries, Ports and Social
Welfare (1980).
Column (3): Government of India (1971).

Female age at marriage

Although there continues to be disagreement among demographers on whether or not small changes in the female age at marriage exercise a major influence on the birth rate, according to a recent study of the demographic trends in Kerala during the period 1959 to 1971, changes in the nuptiality rate (which is significantly related to age at marriage) accounted for as much as 70 per cent of the decline in the fertility rate during that period (F.A.O., 1978, p. 61). The higher age at marriage evidently reflects itself in the proportion of women actually married. Thus, while in the country as a whole, 70 per cent of the rural women in the age group 15–19 were married in 1969, the

21

corresponding percentage was only 30 per cent for Kerala. Also, it cannot be ignored that this increase in the female age at marriage could have had a positive effect on the health status of women and children. Women exposed to childbearing at tender ages seem to show higher frequencies of stillbirths and loss of first-order births. Also, such women have an increased risk of maternal mortality.

As can be seen from Table II.10, the age at marriage for women has always been higher in Kerala State than in the rest of the country.

Table II.10   Mean female age at marriage in Kerala and India,
1901–10 to 1961–70

Decade	Kerala	India
1901–1910	17.13	13.2
1911–1920	17.35	13.6
1921–1930	17.80	12.6
1931–1940	19.66	15.0
1941–1950	19.33	15.4
1951–1960	19.85	16.1
1961–1970	20.88	17.2

Sources: 1. Kerala State, Bureau of Economics and Statistics (1978).
2. Government of India (1975).

It can be noted also that the female age at marriage in Kerala has been rising from decade to decade so that the average for the state was already close to 21 years in 1971. As for the female age at marriage among fishing communities, information at the disaggregated level is unfortunately not available. So, it is not possible to say whether girls from fishing households tend to marry earlier or later than girls from other households in the state.

Marital fertility and family planning

Assuming that changes in marital fertility can occur principally as a result of conscious control, the extent of decline in fertility should depend crucially on the proportion of married couples practising such control. According to information available on the spread of contraception in Kerala State, while about 4 per cent of the eligible couples were practising fertility control in 1965, the proportion had risen to about 26 per cent in 1975–76, and to over 40 per cent in 1980–81 (see Table II.11). Of the total number of couples protected by various methods of contraception, 89 per cent relied on sterilisation in 1981.

22

Table II.11 Percentage of couples protected by various family planning methods in Kerala State

Year	Number of couples at mid-year (in millions)	Number of couples protected (in millions)	Percentage protected by			
			Sterili-sation	IUD	Other methods	Total
1965–66	2.74	0.12	3.69	0.65	–	4.34
1970–71	3.07	0.48	12.37	2.86	0.31	15.54
1975–76	3.44	0.89	23.82	2.02	–	25.84
1979–80	3.50	1.90	29.80	1.18	0.26	31.24

Source: Kerala State, Bureau of Economics and Statistics (1977). Figures for 1979–80 were obtained from an unpublished document of the State Bureau.

Characteristics of sterilisations

As can be seen from Table II.12, of the sterilisations performed between 1970–71 and 1979–80, male sterilisations account for 50 per cent of the total. In the preceding decade of 1960 to 1969, however, male sterilisations accounted for 79 per cent of the total sterilisations performed in the state. In more recent years, there is an

Table II.12 Male, female and total sterilisations in Kerala State, 1960–61 to 1979–80

Year	Male sterili-sations	Female sterili-sations	Total num-ber of sterili-sations	Female steri-lisations as percentage of the total
1960–69	264,673	69,835	334,508	20.9
1970–79	526,139	533,296	1,059,435	50.3
1976–77	129,829	84,566	214,395	39.4
1977–78	15,188	67,225	82,413	81.6
1978–79	15,190	75,092	90,282	83.2
1979–80	14,335	84,691	99,026	85.6

Source: Kerala State, Planning Board (1960–80).

even more noticeable shift towards female sterilisations. During the period 1977–78 to 1979–80, over 80 per cent of the total sterilisations in the state were female sterilisations.

There is evidence that women in Kerala have tended to go in for sterilisation at an earlier age than men. On the whole the percentage of younger people accepting sterilisation has steadily been increasing; among the sterilised persons, the percentage of women who underwent the operation before completing the age of 30 was already as high as 66.7 in 1973–74 as against 48.8 for men undergoing sterilisation. The corresponding percentages for the period 1957–67 were 44.5 for women and 8.1 for men undergoing sterilisation (see Table II.13).

Table II.13   Percentage of sterilised persons according to age and sex in Kerala, 1967–68, 1970–71, 1973–74

	AGE										
Year	15–19		20–24		25–29		30–34		35–39		40+	
	M	F	M	F	M	F	M	F	M	F	M	F
1967–68	–	0.3	0.6	12.1	9.3	37.1	21.6	22.9	28.6	16.8	39.9	3.7
1970–71	0.1	0.1	2.1	17.7	16.1	38.3	24.3	26.8	27.1	14.2	30.3	3.7
1973–74	–	0.4	1.6	23.1	19.9	43.1	27.3	21.1	27.9	10.5	23.2	1.1

M = Male, F = Female

Source: Keralá State, Bureau of Economics and Statistics (1978).

The percentage of persons accepting sterilisation after having three or fewer living children has been on the increase (see Table II.14).While the percentage of such persons was 25.4 in 1957–61, it had risen to 55.3 in 1973–74. As between the sexes, while the average number of living children was 3.29 for a sterilised man, it was 3.71 for a sterilised woman in 1973–74. Also, over the years, there was a noticeable falling trend in the average number of living children per sterilised woman as well as man in Kerala. By 1973–74, as many as 20.5 per cent of persons opting for sterilisation had only two or fewer living children.

Table II.14 Percentage distribution of sterilised persons according to
number of children living in Kerala, 1967–68, 1970–71,
1973–74

Year	One child	Two children	Three or more children
1967–68	0.9	14.9	26.9
1970–71	1.2	19.5	28.7
1973–74	1.4	19.1	34.8

Source: Kerala State, Bureau of Economics and Statistics (1978).

Religious factor in sterilisations

Studies by the state's Demographic Research Centre of the distribution of
sterilised persons by major religious groups showed that while the acceptance of
sterilisation among the Hindus was higher, it was particularly low among the Muslims.
However, while acceptance of sterilisation seems to have been increasing among the
Muslims, it seems to be declining somewhat among the Christians. Table II.15 brings
out these trends.

Table II.15 Percentage distribution of sterilisations by religion,
1961, 1970–71 to 1973–74

Year	Religion		
	Hindus	Christians	Muslims
1961	74.2	20.2	5.2
1970–71	72.4	19.3	8.4
1971–72	67.0	23.9	9.1
1972–73	70.9	19.4	9.6
1973–74	72.9	16.1	11.0

Source: Kerala State, Bureau of Economics and Statistics (1977).

Concluding observations

It should be clear from the available demographic indices that population growth
in Kerala has turned the corner already and is beginning to decelerate. Mortality rates
have been low and falling for some decades. Lately, however, birth rates have also

started declining fast enough to bring down the overall growth rate of the state's population. Nonetheless, there still are pockets in the state among its religious and social groups which are yet to join fully the mainstream of events.

This study, which concentrates on a few fishing villages with different religious composition, will examine issues that need attention in order to assimilate not only the fishing population but also other low income groups into these demographic trends. The village profiles and case studies which follow hopefully will throw light in that direction.

CHAPTER III

PROFILE OF PROJECT VILLAGES

This chapter is divided into four parts. The first part attempts to present a total picture of the Project area and compares and contrasts the demographic position as it has evolved over the years since the Project was started in 1953 in the three Project villages. In the subsequent three parts, a short sketch of each of the villages is presented with the focus principally on the fishing households in each village. These sketches will, it is hoped, serve as a useful background to the individual autobiographies which follow this chapter. The chapter concludes with summary observations based on the village profiles and the macro-level information presented in the preceding chapter.

A.   The Project Area

The three fishing villages chosen for the introduction of mechanised fishing, under the Norwegian Aid Programme, are located in the district of Quilon, 10 to 12 kilometres north of Quilon town. The villages are situated along National Highway 47, going south from Ernakulam to Cape Comorin. First comes Puthenthura and then Neendakara. Both of these villages are located on the northern side of the highway bridge, known by the name of Neendakara Bridge, and the third village, Sakthikulangara, comes soon after one crosses the bridge, going southwards. This bridge is built over an inlet from the sea to the backwaters that run continuously almost all along the coast of Kerala. The backwaters are separated and protected from the ocean by land varying in distance between a couple of hundred metres to a couple of kilometres, except for occasional inlets which connect the backwaters to the sea. The vast stretch of water to the east of the bridge is known as Ashtamudi Lake because the water from here branches off into eight inland creeks. As can be seen from the accompanying map 1, Neendakara Bridge is quite central to the Project area.

The three villages, Puthenthura, Neendakara and Sakthikulangara, fall into two *karas*[1], the first two in the kara of Neendakara and the third in the kara of Sakthikulangara. The *karas* are the smallest units for which separate population figures are available from the decennial population censuses.

---

1   One *kara* may cover one or more villages. In Sakthikulangara kara, there is only the village of Sakthikulangara whereas in Neendakara kara there are a number of small villages including Neendakara and Puthenthura. But a *kara* is not an administrative unit. The smallest administrative unit in the countryside is a *panchayat* which again may cover one or more villages.

Map I: Project Area

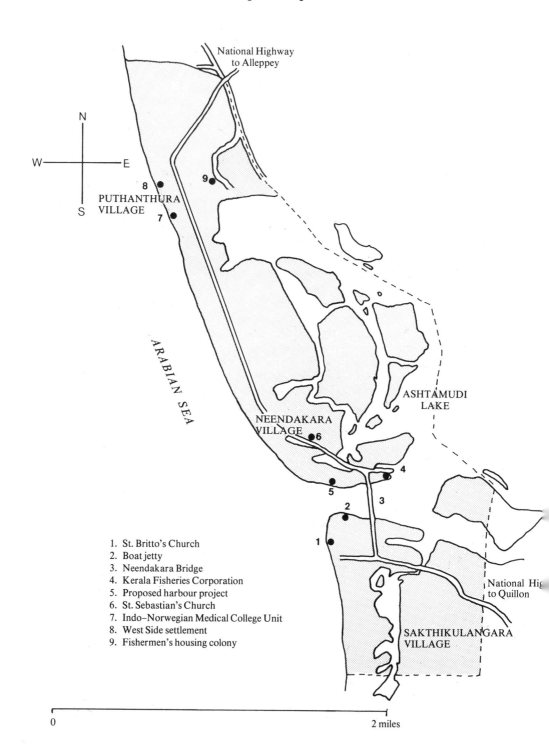

National Highway
to Alleppey

N
W —— E
S

8
PUTHANTHURA
VILLAGE
7

9

ARABIAN SEA

ASHTAMUDI
LAKE

NEENDAKARA
VILLAGE
6

4

5

3

2

1

National Highway
to Quillon

SAKTHIKULANGARA
VILLAGE

1. St. Britto's Church
2. Boat jetty
3. Neendakara Bridge
4. Kerala Fisheries Corporation
5. Proposed harbour project
6. St. Sebastian's Church
7. Indo–Norwegian Medical College Unit
8. West Side settlement
9. Fishermen's housing colony

0   2 miles

Population of the karas

Table III.1 sets out important figures from the censuses relating to the karas of Neendakara and Sakthikulangara. The figures for Neendakara cover Puthenthura also. We can see that while Neendakara was only marginally bigger than Sakthikulangara in 1951, its population in 1971 was larger than that of Sakthikulangara by a little over 38 per cent. Although population figures are not yet forthcoming from the 1981 censuses, there is reason to believe, judging by the expansion in the fishing population to which a reference is made below, the rate of population growth in the decade of 1971–80 also has probably been much higher in Neendakara than in Sakthikulangara.

Table III.1   Population, sex ratio and literacy rates in Sakthikulangara and Neendakara, 1951, 1961 and 1971

	Sakthikulangara			Neendakara		
	1951	1961	1971	1951	1961	1971
Population	5270	6732	8664	5887	8745	11887
Population growth rate		27.7	28.6		48.5	35.9
Sex ratio*	925	943	914	940	958	956
Male literacy rate	56.5	54.1	68.9	60.5	60.4	73.1
Female literacy rate	39.4	36.2	57.1	43.5	53.2	67.7

* Ratio of women to 1,000 men.

Source: Government of India (1951, 1961 and 1971).

It is also worthwhile noting that in both the karas, men outnumber women. But while in Neendakara the sex ratio has been improving over the years, this has not been so in Sakthikulangara. As regards literacy, both the karas have shown not only considerable improvement in the levels of male and female literacy but also a narrowing of the gap between the sexes in this regard. Again, however, the gap is narrower in Neendakara than Sakthikulangara.

Fishing population

The fishing population is concentrated in certain parts of the two karas. In Neendakara, the village of Puthenthura is almost entirely a fishing village. In the village of Neendakara proper, fishermen have been concentrated mostly on the western side of the highway, close to the sea coast, though in recent years, they have spilled over to the east of the highway. Still, on the eastern side mostly non-fishing families live. In Sakthikulangara also, fishing families are concentrated very largely on the western side of the highway.

The decennial censuses do not give separate demographic details about the fishing population. However, on the selection of the above three villages for Norwegian aid, a sample survey was undertaken in 1953 of the localities where fishing families were concentrated. According to this survey, out of a total population in the two karas of about 12,000 the number living by fishing was 3,800, i.e., about 31.7 per cent. After six years, i.e., in 1959, a census was taken of the fishing households of the Project area and it was found that of the total population of 14,217 the fishing population was 4,543, i.e., 32.4 per cent. A subsequent survey in 1963 estimated the fishing population in the Project area as 4,752, forming only 30 per cent of the total population. From the most recent survey conducted in 1978 under the auspices of the State Government of Kerala, it has also been possible to estimate the fishing population of the three villages coming within the Project area. Table III.2 gives these figures along with the comparable information available from earlier surveys and censuses.

Table III.2 Fishing population in Project villages, 1953, 1959, 1963, 1978

Village	1953	1959	1963	1978	Ratio of change between 1953 and 1978 (%)
Sakthikulangara	1,900	2,255	2,204	3,144	65.5
Neendakara	646 }	2,288	2,548 {	3,282	408.0
Puthenthura	1,254			2,607	107.9
Total	3,800	4,543	4,752	9,033	111.9
(Percent of village)	(31.7)	(32.4)	(30.0)	(36.1)	

Note: Figures in brackets are of the total fishing population as a percentage of the total population in the Project area.

Sources: 1. Bog (1954).
2. Indo-Norwegian Project Standing Committee (1960).
3. Indo-Norwegian Project (1964).
4. Unpublished statistics supplied by the Department of Fisheries, Government of Kerala.

It can be seen that over a 25-year period minimum expansion in fishing population has taken place in Sakthikulangara and maximum in Neendakara, the village just across the highway bridge. Also, it would appear that the fishing population grew particularly fast in Neendakara in the 15-year period, 1963 to 1978. Evidently, Neendakara Village has been able to absorb the impact of high immigration into the Project area in the wake of increased economic activity, evidence for which has been quite abundant.

Religious composition of the fishing households

One clear distinction that can be drawn between the fishermen of Sakthikulangara and Neendakara on the one hand, and the fishermen of Puthenthura on the other is in terms of religion. In the former two villages, fishermen are predominantly Christians, belonging to the Latin Catholic church. In the latter village, Puthenthura, though a part of the kara of Neendakara, the fishermen are almost exclusively Hindus. They belong to the Araya caste, a backward caste in the state, whose members specialise in fishing and allied activities. Table III.3 sets out the religious composition of the fishing households in each of the three villages.

Table III.3 Religious composition of fishing households in Project villages, 1978

Village	Total number of households	Christians (Latin Catholics) %	Muslims %	Hindus (Arayas) %	Total %
Sakthikulangara	533	90.0	0.7	9.3	100
Neendakara	564	85.5	0.5	14.0	100
Puthenthura	464	5.1	0.5	94.4	100

Source: Unpublished statistics supplied by the Department of Fisheries, Government of Kerala.

Sex ratio

An aspect of the fishing population of the state as a whole that was mentioned in the preceding chapter is the deficiency of women in fishing households. The 1953 survey of the three Project villages showed that the sex ratio for each of them was rather low. But it was the lowest for the predominantly Hindu fishing village of Puthenthura. However, as can be seen from Table III.4, since 1953 the sex ratio has improved considerably in all three villages. As a result, the sex ratio in 1978 was already higher than the sex ratio for the country as a whole in 1981.

Table III.4   Sex ratio in Project villages, 1953, 1959, 1963, 1978

Village	1953	1959	1963	1978
Sakthikulangara	878	873	868	961
Neendakara	892	} 888	900	938
Puthenthura	858			
Kerala State				
(1) Total				
population	1028		1022	1034
(2) Fishing				
population				975
India	946		941	935

Note: Figures for Kerala State (total population) and India are for the census years, 1951, 1961 and 1981.

Sources: 1. As in Table III.2 for villages.
         2. Government of India (1951, 1961 and 1981) for Kerala State.

Average household size

Table III.5 indicates the change in the size of fishing households over the 25-year period from 1953 to 1978. The factors behind this change are mainly changes in completed family size and in the prevalence of the extended family. The average number of persons per fishing households showed a tendency to increase during the period 1953 to 1963. Thereafter, average household size declined in all three Project villages. Significantly, the decline was greatest in the Hindu village of Puthenthura.

Table III.5   Average size of fishing households in Project villages, 1953, 1959, 1963, 1978

Village	1953	1959	1963	1978
Sakthikulangara	5.6	5.8	6.5	5.9
Neendakara	4.8	} 6.5	6.6	5.8
Puthenthura	6.2			

Note: Separate figures not available for 1959, 1963, 1978.
Source: As for Table III.2

32

Table III.6, giving the distribution of fishing households according to size, confirms the earlier observation about change having affected all three Project villages. While in Sakthikulangara and Neendakara the percentage of households of larger size increased, the same decreased in Puthenthura. The increase was particularly significant in Neendakara where the large or very large households increased from 20 per cent in 1953 to 45 per cent in 1978. Thus, in the predominantly Christian villages of Sakthikulangara and Neendakara, the proportion of households with six persons or less has come down over the 25-year period, 1953 to 1978. The decline is particularly noticeable in Neendakara, the village which, as was noted above, experienced a very sharp increase in its fishing population during the same period. With a great deal of movement of people into this village, possibly the households already existing have had to accommodate friends and relatives on a much larger scale than in the other two villages. In the Hindu village of Puthenthura the percentage of households of six persons or less remained at 65 per cent.

Table III.6 Percentage distribution of fishing households by size in Project villages, 1953, 1978

Household size	Sakthi-kulangara		Neendakara		Puthenthura	
	1953	1978	1953	1978	1953	1978
Small (3 members or less)	13	15	22	10	14	20
Medium (4–6 members)	58	48	58	45	51	45
Large (7–10 members)	25	30	17	31	24	27
Very large (10 or more)	4	7	3	14	11	8
Total	100	100	100	100	100	100

Source: As for Table III.2, sources 1 and 4.

Housing conditions

It is interesting to note that the three Project villages differed from each other in regard to housing conditions right from the start of the Project and that housing differences have continued to persist. This can be seen from Table III.7, which gives the distribution of fishing households by major dwelling types. While only 57 per cent of the fishing households of Sakthikulangara lived in huts in 1953, the corresponding percentages for Neendakara and Puthenthura were 82 and 70 respectively. The percentage of hut dwellers has declined in all three villages, but the lowest percentage still is in Sakthikulangara. It is also significant that in 1978 one out of every four fishing households lived in a *pucca* house. The rate of change in Puthenthura is quite impressive. The percentage of hut dwellers in Puthenthura declined from 70 in 1953 to

48 in 1978. This possibly came about as a result of the choice of the village for a state government project for the construction of 100 new houses for fishermen.

Table III.7   Percentage distribution of fishing households in Project villages by type of dwelling, 1953, 1978

Type of dwelling	Sakthikulangara		Neendakara		Puthenthura	
	1953	1978	1953	1978	1953	1978
Huts	57	37	82	66	70	48
Kutcha	28	36	11	23	21	46*
Pucca	15	27	7	11	9	6*
Total	100	100	100	100	100	100

Note: While huts are made entirely of thatch, *kutcha* houses may have brick or mud walls with thatched roof and *pucca* houses have brick walls with tiled or concrete roofs.

* Strictly speaking, the new houses put up under a government housing scheme for fishermen should be classified as *pucca* since they have brick walls and tiled roofs. If a correction were made for this, the percentage of *kutcha* houses would decline to 23 and that of *pucca* houses would go up to 29.

Source: As for Table III.6.

Literacy ratios

One of the indices ordinarily used for ascertaining the position of a group in the socio-economic scale is the percentage of literates in the population. Since fishermen as a group are known to be backward, it would be expected that their literacy rate would be lower than among the populace as a whole. This, however, is not quite borne out by the information available with respect to the fishing population in the Project area.

According to the information from the decennial censuses of population, as presented in Table III.8, it can be seen that literacy rates were close to or above the corresponding ratios for Quilon District (Rural). In both karas there was also a marked improvement in the female literacy rate during the 20-year period, 1951–1971. In Sakthikulangara, however, the gain in female literacy was achieved entirely in the decade of 1961–1971.

The earliest separate estimate of the literacy rate among fishermen is available for 1959 when, as stated above, a census of fisherfolk of the Project area was conducted under the auspices of the Project authorities. This was followed by a sample survey of the fishermen areas in 1963. The information collected on changes in literacy among the fishing community is given in Table III.9.

Table III.8 Literacy rates (total, male and female) in Project karas and rural Quilon, 1951, 1961, 1971

Village	1951			1961			1971		
	T	M	F	T	M	F	T	M	F
Sakthikulangara	48.3	56.6	39.4	45.5	54.2	36.3	63.3	68.9	57.1
Neendakara	52.3	60.5	43.5	57.8	64.5	53.2	69.0	73.1	64.7
Quilon (Rural)	48.2	57.3	39.3	49.4	57.2	42.7	64.8	69.9	59.6

T = Total, M = Male, F = Female

Source: Government of India (1951, 1961 and 1971).

Table III.9 Literacy rates among fishermen of the Project karas, 1959, 1963

Village	Fishermen						All population		
	1959			1963			1961		
	T	M	F	T	M	F	T	M	F
Sakthikulangara	52.9	61.3	43.3	53.5	62.3	43.4	45.5	54.2	36.3
Neendakara	63.2	68.6	57.1	55.6	60.4	53.3	57.8	64.5	53.2

T = Total, M = Male, F = Female

Sources: 1. Indo-Norwegian Project Standing Committee (1960 and 1963).
2. Government of India (1961).

It can be seen that with respect to Neendakara, literacy rates for 1959 were significantly higher than those for 1963. It is difficult however to accept that within a short period of four years, literacy ratios could have suffered such declines. Since the census results are likely to be more correct than estimates based on a sample survey, the 1959 literacy ratios can be taken to be more accurate. That being so, it is reasonable to say that the literacy rate for the fishing community is not lower than for the total population of each of the karas for both men and women.

For 1978, it has been possible to obtain figures for each of the three villages with respect to the educational status of men and women from the fishing households. Table III.10 sets out these figures. It can be seen that illiteracy is the highest among the fisherfolk of Neendakara village and the lowest in Puthenthura for both men and women. But it is in Sakthikulangara where we note the highest percentage of women as well as men completing the tenth standard and going on to higher education, including

35

university graduation. Interestingly, however, the proportion of men and women having done, or doing, between five to ten years of schooling is the highest, not in Sakthikulangara, but in Puthenthura.

Table III.10 Percentage distribution of fisherfolk of Project villages by sex and educational attainment, 1978

Education	Sakthi-kulangara		Neenda-kara		Puthen-thura	
	Male	Female	Male	Female	Male	Female
Illiterate	21.6	25.5	31.2	41.2	14.2	19.1
Up to Standard V	38.7	41.7	43.9	35.9	39.7	40.3
V to X	32.9	28.7	21.7	20.6	42.4	36.3
X or above	5.3	4.1	3.0	2.1	3.4	3.9
Graduate	1.5	0.5	0.2	0.2	0.3	0.4
Total	100.0	100.0	100.0	100.0	100.0	100.0

Source: As for Table III.3.

Work participation and occupational distribution

It can be seen from Table III.11 that work participation rates are higher for both men and women in Puthenthura than in Sakthikulangara and Neendakara. The gap is particularly noticeable with respect to women.

Table III.11 Male and female work participation rates in Project villages, 1978

Work participation	Sakthi-kulangara		Neenda-kara		Puthen-thura	
	Male	Female	Male	Female	Male	Female
Working	55.2	13.2	53.5	17.2	61.0	44.0
Non-working	44.8	86.8	46.5	82.8	39.0	56.0
Total	100.0	100.0	100.0	100.0	100.0	100.0

Source: As for Table III.3.

It was noted above that illiteracy was also less in Puthenthura. But can higher work participation among women be attributed largely to a higher literacy rate? If so, how does one explain the higher work participation in Neendakara than in Sakthikulangara although the former has a very much lower rate of female literacy? Clearly, differences in literacy rates do not quite explain the inter-village differences in female work participation.

Civil condition

An attempt was made to see if there were any differences between the villages in the civil condition of women who worked. As can be seen from Table III.12, even though in all three villages approximately 70 per cent of the working women are married, the proportion of never-married women in the work force is much higher in Puthenthura than in the other two villages. Is that a reflection of the relative prosperity of the village compared to the other villages? From the earlier survey done by Bog, it was found that most women who took to work were widows or separated. There seems to be a change in this regard in all three villages.

Table III.12 Percentage distribution of working women by civil condition, 1978

Civil condition	Sakthi-kulangara	Neenda-kara	Puthen-thura
Married	79.8	70.1	68.5
Widow/divorced/ separated	13.1	12.4	9.0
Unmarried	7.1	17.5	22.5
Total	100.0	100.0	100.0

Source: As for Table III.3.

Occupational distribution

The distribution of men in both Sakthikulangara and Neendakara from fishing households by nature of their work as presented in Table III.13, shows that while more than 50 per cent of them are engaged in mechanised fishing, only 20 per cent or so are in traditional fishing. In Puthenthura, on the other hand, close to 60 per cent are engaged in traditional fishing and less than 15 per cent in mechanised fishing. Surprisingly the concentration of boat owners in Sakthikulangara is twice that of

Neendakara where also mechanised fishing is common. Those owning mechanised boats in Puthenthura are very few.

Table III.13   Percentage distribution of working fishermen in Project villages by nature of work, 1978

Occupation	Sakthi-kulangara	Neenda-kara	Puthen-thura
I. **Mechanised fishing**	**56.5**	**56.0**	**12.7**
(i) Deck-hands	26.6	32.1	8.9
(ii) Drivers	12.6	15.7	2.8
(iii) Boat owners	17.3	8.2	1.0
II. **Fish businessmen and** **related activities**	**5.8**	**12.0**	**7.2**
III. **Traditional fishing**	**23.0**	**21.3**	**68.1**
(i) Vallom owners	13.1	3.6	10.6
(ii) Wage workers	9.0	9.1	56.7
(iii) Net casters	0.2	8.3	0.1
(iv) Net makers	0.7	0.3	0.7
IV. **Permanent employment**	**13.5**	**7.2**	**9.4**
V. **Others** (tailors, tea shop)	**1.2**	**3.5**	**2.6**
Total	100.0	100.0	100.0

Source: As for Table III.3.

Not only is boat ownership concentrated in Sakthikulangara, but its distribution pattern is quite uneven. It can be seen from Table III.14 that 86 per cent of the mechanised boats owned in the Project area are owned by the people in Sakthikulangara. But of the boats owned in Sakthikulangara, close to 60 per cent are owned by persons owning two or more boats. In Neendakara and Puthenthura combined, on the other hand, the corresponding proportion is 19 per cent. It would be reasonably safe to say, therefore, that while Sakthikulangara has benefited more from the mechanisation of boats, economic inequalities have at the same time increased.

The distribution of working fisherwomen by nature of their work (see Table III.15) shows that in Puthenthura, the village with the highest female work participation, the activity which occupies almost 70 per cent of these women is net making. In the other two villages, net making is an activity of only peripheral interest. On the other hand, the activity which occupies most working women in Sakthikulangara and Neendakara is dealership in prawns.

Table III.14 Ownership distribution of mechanised boats in Project
villages, 1978

Number of boats owned	Sakthi-kulangara**	Neenda-kara	Puthen-thura
1) Owning one boat*	149	43	4
2) Owning two boats	65	1	2
3) Owning three boats	13	–	–
4) Owning four boats	6	–	–
5) Owning five boats	3	1	–
Number of boat owners**	236	45	6
Number of boats owned	360	51	8
	(36)	(12)	(8)

* Households owning only part of a boat could not be identified separately because in cases of joint
  ownership a boat, it appears, is registered in one name only. It is, therefore, very likely that the actual
  number of boat owners may be very much larger, particularly in the category of those owning one boat.
** The ownership of boats in Sakthikulangara refers to the whole panchayat and is not confined just to
  the Project village.

Source: Data collected for the study.

Table III.15 Percentage distribution of working women from fishing households
in Project villages by nature of work, 1978

Occupation	Sakthi-kulangara	Neenda-kara	Puthen-thura
Net maker	4.0	6.5	68.9
Prawn processor for wages	26.3	23.0	24.0
Coir processing for fibring	2.0	0.5	2.1
Prawn dealer	44.5	35.9	0.5
Prawn peeler at home	2.0	8.8	0.1
Fish business	–	–	0.5
Shell collector	–	4.6	–
Fish headload vendor	17.2	7.8	0.6
Others	4.0	7.4	3.3
Permanent employment	–	5.5	–
Total	100.0	100.0	100.0

Source: Data collected for the study.

While both net making and prawn dealing can be considered activities of the self-employed, the former is much lower paid than the latter. In all three villages around one-fourth of the working fisherwomen are engaged in prawn processing for wages but the absolute number drawn from Puthenthura is almost as large as the number drawn from the other two villages together. Fishing of prawns has, as has been noted in the very first chapter, emerged as a major economic activity almost entirely as a result of mechanised fishing. It can be seen that though only a small number of men from Puthenthura are engaged directly in mechanised fishing, the jobs it has generated in prawn processing have attracted quite a considerable number from Puthenthura. Prawn dealership, on the other hand, has been the preserve of only women from the fishing households of Sakthikulangara and Neendakara. Interestingly, at the same time, headload fish vending, a low income-cum-status job, is almost non-existent in Puthenthura due to a relatively small non-fishing population and thus a lack of vending opportunities.

We have tried to compare the changes that have occurred in each of the villages over a span of a quarter century after the Project was initiated. It is quite apparent that the changes that have occurred in each of the villages are not quite the same. In what follows, we try to give a brief description of each of the villages and to highlight its main characteristics.

B. Sakthikulangara Village

Sakthikulangara does not really fit the description of a village any longer, judged by the facilities to which it has access. Apart from its being easily accessible by both long and short distance bus services, a host of taxis are always waiting at the bridge junction. Also, the infrastructural development in and around the village gives it the feel of a town.

As one approaches Sakthikulangara from the south, the roads branching off on either side, i.e., east and west of the National Highway are scattered with modern cement concrete structures. On the east side, one sees a series of well stocked shops, quite a few of which deal exclusively in spare parts for mechanised crafts, with a good sprinkling of shops and parlours selling liquor which, though manufactured within India, carries foreign names such as whisky, rum, gin and brandy. Five commercial banks have put up their branch offices also on the east side. Going north, as one gets closer to Ashtamudi Lake, one comes to a number of peeling and fish-drying sheds. On the bank of the lake itself is the private boat jetty belonging to a major fish exporting firm, controlled by one of the local families that has prospered in recent years. There is also the government boat-building yard run by the Department of Fisheries. It was put up by the Norwegians in 1954–55 and is said to be quite well equipped. It has a mechanical workshop and a modern carpentry unit. Mechanised boats up to 11 metres in length are constructed and repaired here. There are over a half-dozen private mechanical workshops and also a private boat yard in the village.

On the west side also there are a number of modern structures but most of them are residential buildings with far fewer shops than on the east side. Coming up north from Quilon city by the highway, the stench of fish is overwhelming as one comes close to the highway bridge. Fish and prawn peel are dried indiscriminately close to the sidewalks on the west side. A few metres before the bridge stands a building which looks like frosted cake with several layers. It is a monument dedicated to Virgin Mary, by a local fisherman who virtually rose from rags to riches. The Parish Church is also located on the west side, close to the sea coast, in the very heart of what was once the hub of fishing activity. This was when all fishing was undertaken in traditional crafts.

The monument to Virgin Mary is now the nerve centre of the village. All men and women looking for casual work hang around here. Also, during the peak fishing season, you see innumerable trucks and cyclists positioned on the sides waiting to transport the fish catch to various places. In addition, a host of people can be seen here going to or from the public boat jetty on the west side. These may be auctioneers, commission agents, deck hands, dealers in fish including prawn, fish sorters or prawn peelers. Not all of these persons belong to Sakthikulangara village. Many come from Neendakara, Puthenthura and several other neighbouring villages, particularly during the peak fishing months of June to September.

The public boat jetty

The boat jetty located on the west side is the centre of feverish activity, particularly during the peak months. Though the land immediately jutting on water is largely government property, families owning adjacent lands have virtually taken possession of government land. Unless one is familiar with the place, one is bound to be utterly confused by what is occurring here. While several people are running to and fro with fish baskets and ice slabs on their heads on extremely wet and slippery terrain you see women sitting in groups on the same ground sorting out catch as it is unloaded. An assortment of fish, mostly of poor species, gets caught along with prawns. Sorting out the catch is itself a major preoccupation of some women here.

The jetty proper is even more confusing. Every time a boat unloads its catch, people rush towards it. Each basketful of catch is auctioned separately. There is always an auctioner at hand with his notebook and pencil. There is always more than one boat landing its catch at the same time. Each auctioneer is surrounded by people and in each such group every one seems to be shouting at the same time. The auctioneer, who is evidently familiar with every face around him, knows what the bid is and from whom. The whole bidding is based on the judgement of the eye. So one has to be quite experienced in judging the contents of a basket. Some groups are altogether male, others almost entirely female in composition. Men go for bigger and expensive lots whereas women dealers go for less expensive lots. So both men and women go about with a lot of liquid cash tucked at the waist in their wrap-around *mundus*. As each basket is auctioned, it is taken aside for sorting right on the jetty or if it is sorted already, it is moved to a peeling shed for processing. Quite a few peeling sheds have been put up by the side of the jetty. But there are several which are located away from the jetty.

It is a public jetty, but since land immediately adjacent to the landing site is owned by some twelve fishing families of the village, it is to these families that the whole of the jetty virtually seems to belong. They have built their own peeling sheds and rent them out. One of these families has put up a petrol pump to serve the boats. Another family has put up an ice factory. It is one of the 17 ice factories located in this village.

41

Also, there are innumerable tea shops and agency booths. The latter have been set up in rented premises by the processing and/or export firms. The jetty owners make good income by way of rent they charge for these booths. They also collect a fee from not only every boat that comes to berth there, but also auction agents and dealers who use their peeling sheds. No wonder that these families have become very prosperous over the years since mechanisation was introduced. But they have done little to improve the jetty or its surroundings. Today, it is not only a highly disorderly place but also most unhygienic, particularly in the peak season.

While the trawlers, which bring in prawns, start berthing in the afternoon, the boats that berth at the jetty in the forenoon are gill netters and drift netters which bring in catches comprising sharks, catch fish, seer, tuna and tuna-like species, scianids, perches, pomfrets, etc. These catches are also auctioned as they are landed. The quantities landed can be quite substantial during the peak season and have to be dispatched promptly to various centres of consumption in and outside the district for retail sale by local vendors. A large proportion of the fish other than prawns from the jetty finds its way to the bicycles and lorries standing outside. There are very few women headload vendors. The bicycles transport fish to markets within 25 to 30 kilometres, while lorries carry it over much longer distances inland of up to 150 kilometres.

The use of ice has expanded phenomenally in recent years. Almost the entire quantity of prawn landed at Sakthikulangara region is exported. The use of ice is of crucial importance right from the time prawns are landed to the time they are ready to be frozen to avoid spoilage. It is estimated that, in weight, the ratio of ice needed to preserve prawns is 3:2. For other varieties of fish the ratio of ice required in terms of weight is less. Given the scale of requirement, ice is a very scarce commodity during the peak season.

Electricity connection

Not only is Sakthikulangara well provided with street lights but also the proportion of households with electricity is quite impressive. Most of the modern structures, residential and non-residential, have electricity, as do even several of the modest structures built partially or altogether of thatch. According to the latest panchayat statistics, there are 568 street lights in the whole of the area within its jurisdiction. Since the proportion of brick houses in the panchayat is about 27 per cent assuming that at least each such house has electricity, it means that at a minimum every fourth house in the Panchayat has access to electricity. The ratio is in all probability much higher, particularly for the village of Sakthikulangara which is the centre of economic activity in the panchayat.

Drinking water

There are two sources of water supply, wells and pipes. Many of the fishing households have wells. Since most of the area is only about two metres above sea level, the water table is quite high. As a result, digging of wells is not expensive. However, the well water has been found to have a very high level of salinity. Also, it is not considered safe in other respects. The normal practice, therefore, is to use well water for washing and cleaning purposes and depend on public taps for drinking water.

One of the very first things that the Norwegians did under their aid project was to connect all three villages they were covering, as well as the town of Quilon, with safe drinking water from the fresh water lake known by the name Sasthancottah. Water is filtered and pumped through pipes. Thus Sakthikulangara has had access to safe water supply since 1955. Initially, some 45 public taps were located at strategic points so that safe water was within easy reach for most of the households. Thus, over 70 per cent of the houses were within a distance of 200 metres or less from a public tap.

Toilet facilities

One thing that the panchayat as a whole, and the village in particular, lack is sufficient toilet and drainage facilities. There are no public toilets or latrines in the panchayat. In the early phase of the project, some 800 latrines were built free for private households, but there was very little enthusiasm for using them. Having been used from time immemorial to bathing in public and defecating in farms and other open spaces, people's reaction was understandable. In recent years, however, practically all the modern houses built in the area have latrines as well as bathrooms. This can be taken as an indication of a change in attitudes.

Financial institutions and sources of credit

Sakthikulangara village is well provided with banking and other financing institutions. Two major commercial banks in the nationalised banking sector, Central Bank of India and State Bank of Travancore, have set up their branches here. In addition, the Kerala Financial Corporation, a state government institution, has an office here meant to help fishermen with long-term credit. Also, three banks from the relatively smaller private banking sector operate their branches in Sakthikulangara. In addition, 15 registered indigenous saving associations, known as chit funds, operate here. These are apart from many more unregistered chit funds that people operate.

Thus, there are many sources of credit available in the village. The banks give loans mostly for commercial purposes although loans for larger periods are not altogether ruled out by them. Loans taken from commercial banks for the purchase of mechanised boats are generally for a four-year period. In fact, all the banks have schemes under which loans are extended to weaker sections of the community on concessional terms. The current rate of interest charged by the banks works out to between 18 and 20 per cent but for concessional finance, the rates vary from 4 to 16 per cent. Also bank loans are ordinarily granted against adequate security, but for concessional finance, banks make some relaxations. That is how fishermen engaged in traditional fishing and women engaged in running peeling sheds or doing prawn business are able to avail themselves of bank finance. There seems to be a general awareness in the village, among working men as well as women, about the facilities various banks are offering and their terms and people do not hesitate to use them as and when they become eligible.

The most popular credit institution, however, is the chit fund, a traditional source of saving and borrowing within the community. These funds operate various schemes, the most common being auction chitty and kuri chitty. In auction chitty, the member offering the highest discount is entitled to draw the amount, against acceptable security. The auction is generally restricted to contributing members only. In kuri chitty, on the other hand, lots are drawn between members at regular intervals and the successful member can draw the amount against acceptable security. There is also the rolling system under which you take a loan and repay it every day. Chitty is a very active business, not only in this village, but also in most other villages. Practically all earning members of a household become members of one chitty or another. But most chitties are unregistered and operate on the trust members repose in their managers.

There is no professional money lender in the village, but that does not mean that no private money lending takes place here. Many shop keepers are known to do a certain amount of money lending in addition to the credit they extend on the goods they sell. Also, a certain amount of lending takes place between not only boat owners and their crew, but also households. Gold ornaments are usually acceptable in mortgage for transactions between households.

Educational facilities

The Church, which was established here in 1878, has been taking a leading role in providing and expanding educational facilities. The first primary school was established here in 1899 and this was upgraded in 1923 when it had a strength of 400 students. In 1949, a high school was started by the Church. Given the facilities within the village, embracing primary, secondary and high school, it has been quite easy for any one so desiring to attain the level of a school-leaving certificate without leaving the village. Nevertheless, education in Sakthikulangara is not well dispersed. Firstly, there are still wide disparities between men and women. Secondly, the proportion of illiterates among men as well as women is higher in Sakthikulangara than its two neighbouring villages of Neendakara and Puthenthura, though the latter are not so well provided with educational facilities. At the same time, there is a high proportion of men reaching higher levels of education.

Medical facilities

Right in the village, there are three private dispensaries and three private hospitals. There is also an Ayurvedic dispensary. However, two public hospitals, the Project Health Centre and Quilon District Hospital, also are within easy reach. The former is located at a distance of four kilometres to the north and the latter is located about 10 kilometres to the south. Both of them can be reached by bus, scooter or taxi. Many people from this village go to the Quilon District Hospital which is the oldest hospital in the district, established as early as 1870. Quilon town has also a number of private as well as Mission hospitals.

The church in Sakthikulangara

Though the village derives its name from the local Hindu temple devoted to goddess Sakthi, its fishing population is entirely Christian by religion and, as was stated above, belongs to the Latin Catholic denomination. The Parish Church was established in 1878 and its influence on the personal and social relations within the community has continued to be strong and pervasive ever since. What is of particular importance in the context of the present study is that not only is the Church involved in all the vital events of life, viz., birth, marriage, and death, it also keeps a record of these events.

The church records

In fact, the church in Sakthikulangara maintains separate registers not only to record baptisms, burials, and marriages, but also to record 'changes in each family'. In addition, there is the annual return book to draw a balance sheet, as it were, of the demographic events among the village Latin Catholics on the completion of every year. Access to these registers was found to be of immense help in gaining insight into the demographic changes among the fishing households of Sakthikulangara in spite of certain limitations of the information.

Births and deaths

Table III.16 sets out birth and death rates, for the last thirty years, for Sakthikulangara Parish. As will readily be seen, recorded birth rates have been very high in the Parish, exceeding 40 births per 1,000 of population from 1950 to 1974.

Table III.16 Birth and death rates in Sakthikulangara
Parish, 1950–1979

Period	Birth rate	Death rate
1950–1954	46.5	8.6
1955–1959	45.4	8.1
1960–1964	39.0	5.8
1965–1969	42.6	5.7
1970–1974	40.7	5.8
1975–1979	31.2	4.9

Source: St. John Britto Church, Parish Records.

It is only during 1975–79 that a decline in the recorded birth rate can clearly be discerned. On the other hand, the recorded death rate in the Parish has been very low right from the beginning and became even lower from 1960 onwards. There is need, however, to be a little cautious here. Strictly speaking, all births in Christian

45

households are required to go through baptism and therefore to be recorded in the church register, but the possibility cannot be ruled out that some births do not get recorded. Infant deaths occurring before baptism often go unrecorded according to the Parish priests past and present. The extent to which births are unrecorded has been estimated on the basis of the information collected for the purpose of this study from randomly selected fisherfolk households in each of the three villages with regard to total pregnancies and infant deaths over three generations. For the five-year period 1975–79, corrected birth and death rates would work out to 34.7 and 8.4 instead of 31.2 and 4.9 respectively. Therefore, while there can be no doubt that both birth and death rates have experienced substantial declines in recent years, it is doubtful that actual rates are as low as the church records show.

In addition to information on the number of births occurring in a household the church record in Sakthikulangara also shows the place of delivery. Until 1970, when delivery took place in an institution, the name of institution was also recorded. On the basis of the information thus available, Table III.17 has been constructed setting out the distribution of recorded births on the basis of the place of delivery and type of institution. It can be seen that the shift of deliveries from home to hospital started only in the 1950s and that this shift was almost complete by the end of the 1970s. This should, by any standard, be considered a phenomenally rapid change.

Table III.17 Distribution of births in Sakthikulangara by place of delivery and type of institution, 1950–1979

| Period | Home | Hospital | Public hospital | | Private hospital | |
			Govt hospital	Foundation hospital*	Mission hospital	Private hospital
1950–54	98.2	1.8	1.6	–	0.2	–
1955–59	87.7	12.3	4.2	7.0	1.1	–
1960–64	68.1	31.9	5.4	21.8	4.7	–
1965–69	46.5	53.5	12.5	24.6	10.4	5.8
1970–74	13.1	86.9	NA	NA	NA	NA
1975–79	3.7	96.3	NA	NA	NA	NA

* The hospital put up under the Norwegian Aid Programme is commonly referred to in the Project Area as Foundation Hospital. Its present formal name is the Indo-Norwegian Medical College Unit, Neendakara.

NA = Not available

Source: St. John Britto Church, Parish Records.

Choice of institution

Other studies of low income communities in Kerala suggest that a shift of deliveries from home to institutions could be a major factor in gaining acceptance of family planning for various reasons (Gulati, 1980). One important reason, it is felt, is that since institutional care improves the survival rates of infants, it indirectly helps the acceptance of a smaller family size. At the same time, however, the influence of the hospital doctors and other staff on the patients is found to make an important difference, though this depends on the type of hospital. Doctors and other staff in hospitals run by Christian organisations, particularly those of Catholic persuasion, are not supposed to promote the adoption of family planning. The question of such hospitals performing sterilisations hardly arises. It is therefore only to be expected that where deliveries take place in mission hospitals, there may be a certain delay in acceptance of family planning.

It can be seen from Table III.17 that during the five-year period, 1965–69, the period for which latest distribution of recorded hospital deliveries by type of institution is available, 30 per cent of such deliveries occurred in private mission hospitals. Of these, nine out of ten were mission hospitals.

Of the deliveries occurring in public hospitals, two-thirds or more were in the Project hospital. This in all probability was the result of the intensive field work undertaken by the staff of this hospital, particularly in its early years when the Norwegians were in charge. Evidently, at least initially, a considerable amount of ground work was necessary for the people to be brought around to realising the usefulness of institutional care at the time of delivery. Acceptance of family planning only follows thereafter.

Age at marriage

Sakthikulangara's fisherfolk present an interesting situation combining virtually total acceptance of institutional care of their recorded deliveries with what is, by the standard of Kerala State, a rather low age at first marriage of women.

Table III.18 sets out the mean age at first marriage for both men and women in Sakthikulangara Parish from 1901 to 1980. It can be seen that the age at marriage of women in Sakthikulangara was 16.20 in 1901–10 when the corresponding figure for Kerala State as a whole was 17.13. In 1961–70, the corresponding figures were 17.13 for Sakthikulangara and 20.88 for Kerala State. Thus while for Kerala State as a whole the age at marriage of women increased by 3.75 years during the period 1901–10 to 1961–70, it increased by only 1.51 years for Sakthikulangara Parish. As a result, the gap between the mean age at marriage of women for Kerala State and that for Sakthikulangara Parish has widened from 0.93 years in 1901–10 to 3.15 years.

47

Table III.18 Mean age at first marriage in Sakthikulangara Parish, 1901–1979

Year	Male age at marriage	Female age at marriage
1901–10	24.00	16.20
1911–20	24.23	16.34
1921–30	23.59	16.32
1931–40	25.08	17.28
1941–50	24.72	17.61
1951–60	24.63	17.25
1961–70	24.94	17.73
1971–79	25.31	17.71

Source: St. John Britto's Church, Parish Records.

III. Neendakara Village

Between Sakthikulangara and Neendakara villages lies the Neendakara bar, which is now spanned by a modern highway bridge, known as the Neendakara Bridge. In Malayalam language, Neendakara means a long bank. Right from early days, Neendakara was the point of entry and exit for wooden ships carrying cargoes to or from the interior. When the Portuguese established their trading settlement in Quilon, some ten kilometres south, their ships had to pass through Neendakara bar. St. Sebastian Church in Neendakara village, still the most outstanding building, was put up by the Portuguese in 1588.

Going north from Sakthikulangara, as one crosses the highway bridge, one cannot miss the Church to the east, which is now being rebuilt on quite a massive scale. However, before one reaches the Church there are on the eastern side two rather large modern buildings. One houses the government-owned freezing plant and ice factory. These are run by a public sector firm, Kerala Fisheries Corporation. The firm has a small jetty of its own where the trawlers find their own berth and land their catch. The second building belongs to a privately-owned exporting firm which also has its own freezing plant, ice factory and landing jetty.

Unlike Sakthikulangara, on the Neendakara side of the lake there is no public jetty to which individual fishermen are allowed easy access. They have to go to the public jetty in Sakthikulangara, regardless of whether the fisherman owning the boat belongs to Sakthikulangara, Neendakara or anywhere else. Had there been a public jetty on the Neendakara side also, congestion would have been far less in Sakthikulangara. Unfortunately, the state government's plan to put up a public jetty on the Neendakara side seems to have bogged down along with the more ambitious project for a fishing harbour.

On the western side, immediately after one steps out of the highway bridge, there is a vast space between the sea and the highway, which is now cordoned off by a high wall for the proposed fisheries harbour. Neendakara is already classified as a minor port, handling the export of ilmenite sand and the import of raw cashew-nuts. A permanent office of the Dredging Superintendent is located on the harbour site to undertake regular dredging operations so that the lighters and barges can move freely through the channel. The channel is kept deep enough for small mechanised fishing boats also to move freely.

Economic integration of the two villages

Earlier in this chapter, it was stated that over the past 25 years, the fishing population expanded most in Neendakara and least in Sakthikulangara. It was noted also that the fishing population of Neendakara grew particularly fast in the past 15 years, 1963 to 1978, possibly because the village was in a position to absorb the maximum impact of the immigration into the Project area in the wake of the increased economic activity related to fishing. In fact, given the extent of involvement of the fishing households from either side of the highway bridge in mechanised fishing, and allowing for the fact that so far practically all the boats have to berth and land their catches on the Sakthikulangara side, it would be quite reasonable to ask if they should not be considered as one composite group. Several men and women from Neendakara go in large numbers to work for the mechanised boats, be they trawlers or gill netters, plying to and from the public jetty in Sakthikulangara. Those engaged in buying and selling of fish including prawns also have to go to the public jetty in Sakthikulangara. Such also is the case with most of those working as casual sorters of fish or peelers of prawns. Likewise, not all the persons, men and women, working in the freezing plants and ice factories located in Neendakara are residents of the village. Quite a few live in Sakthikulangara, and also in Puthenthura. Similarly, while there exist two bank offices in Neendakara, several persons from Neendakara have their accounts and dealings with the banks across the bridge. In the same way, not only various commercial establishments but also schools, colleges and hospitals in Sakthikulangara cannot be considered as out of easy reach of the residents of Neendakara. Still, there are some clear differences between the two villages.

Points of difference

The fishing families in Neendakara, as has been pointed out already, are much more modestly housed. While one out of every four fishing households in Sakthikulangara is living in a pucca house, this is so only for one out of every ten fishing households in Neendakara. The vast majority live in thatched huts or kutcha houses. Also, while the involvement of both the villages in mechanised fishing was equally large, it was found that the concentration of boat owners (i.e., the proportion of

49

those owning mechanised craft) was twice as large in Sakthikulangara. In fact, not only is the proportion of households owning mechanised craft much smaller in Neendakara than in Sakthikulangara, but also the boat ownership in Neendakara, with a few exceptions, is much more modest. Thus, while close to 60 per cent of the boat owners in Sakthikulangara own two or more boats, in Neendakara, the corresponding percentage of such boat owners is only four. Also, again relatively speaking, there are far more illiterates, men as well as women, in Neendakara than in Sakthikulangara. So, Neendakara fishermen are, it would appear, only poor cousins of the fishermen in Sakthikulangara, however integrated may be the economies of the two villages now.

Economic and social infrastructure

Neendakara village is well provided with street lighting. The source of protected water is the same as Sakthikulangara, namely the fresh water lake at Sasthancottah, some thirty kilometres away. Almost all fishing households live at a distance of less than 200 metres from the nearest public water tap. The government hospital nearest to Neendakara is the one that was established under the Norwegian Aid Programme. It is located about 2 kilometres to the north and can be reached by bus in less than ten minutes. Apart from a small mission hospital and a private dispensary in Neendakara itself, private hospitals and dispensaries across the bridge in Sakthikulangara are also within easy reach of the people of Neendakara.

As regards educational facilities, Neendakara is reasonably well provided. The village has two upper primary and five lower primary schools. The most important school here is the St. Agnes Upper Primary School, a co-educational institution, run directly under the Bishop of Quilon. The school has been in existence since 1951. It works in two shifts now. If, in spite of the educational facilities within its reach, Neendakara is more backward in terms of literacy than Sakthikulangara, the reason for this has to be found somewhere else.

Births and deaths

St. Sebastian Church of Neendakara has been in existence for almost 400 years now and some of its records possibly go back to the year the Church was put up. Access could, therefore, be gained easily to its records for recent years. Table III.19 sets out birth and death rates for Neendakara Parish for the last 30 years. As can be seen, the comparison of recorded birth rates in the first and last quinquennium shows a decline of the order of 35 per cent in the course of a 25-year period. But the figures for the intervening quinquennia do not indicate the rate of decline. On the other hand, it would appear that the decline in the recorded death rate, as yielded by the comparison of the figures for the first and the last quinquennia, somewhat understates the actual situation.

Table III.19   Birth and death rates in Neendakara Parish, 1950–79

Period	Birth rate	Death rate
1950–54	55.0	9.20
1955–59	48.1	5.1
1960–64	51.7	8.5
1965–69	46.2	4.7
1970–74	49.8	8.2
1975–79	36.1	8.1

Source: St. SebastianChurch, Parish Records.

While discussing the figures obtained for Sakthikulangara Parish, a suspicion was expressed that the church records there possibly did not record births of children dying before their baptism. What, if at all, was the recording error for such births in the records of the Neendakara Parish?

First, when one compares uncorrected figures for Neendakara with those of Sakthikulangara, the former are already considerably higher. Second, on the basis of the information collected from selected families in Neendakara in regard to infant deaths and pregnancies the correction factor that could be applied to its recorded figures cannot exceed five per cent. The corrected birth and death rates for the period 1975 to 1979 would then work out to 38.0 and 10.0 respectively as against the corresponding figures for Sakthikulangara of 34.7 and 8.4.

As in Sakthikulangara, church records in Neendakara indicate the place of delivery of recorded births. In fact, where a delivery has taken place in an institution the records in Neendakara have continued to give the name of the institution even after 1970. Table III.20 gives therefore the distribution of recorded births on the basis of the place of delivery and type of institution. It can be seen that for the period 1950 to 1969, very few (less than five per cent) of the deliveries took place in hospitals; the real shift seems to have started only in the 1970s, when close to half of the recorded deliveries had already shifted to hospitals. In Sakthikulangara it will be recalled, the shift of that order had already been achieved during the quinquennium, 1965 to 1969.

Of the deliveries from Neendakara which took place in hospitals during 1975–79, only 20 per cent were accounted for by public hospitals, with the share of the Foundation hospital being just one per cent. Almost three-fourths of the hospital deliveries were accounted for by mission hospitals. In Sakthikulangara, of the hospital deliveries in 1965–69, while 70 per cent were accounted for by public hospitals, with the share of the Foundation hospital being 46 per cent, mission hospitals could account for less than 20 per cent. Can the larger share of mission hospitals in Neendakara's hospital deliveries be connected in some way to the stronger influence of the church on the fishing households of Neendakara? Or could it be that people feel safer with mission hospitals than public hospitals? While public hospitals offer virtually free services, this is not altogether true with respect to mission hospitals. In this context, it is relevant to note that, according to the view generally encountered among the common folk in the Project area, the quality of service provided by the Foundation hospital has deteriorated since the Norwegians left the scene in the mid-1960s. How far the observation with respect to the quality of service is valid is difficult to document. It is probably still true that the earlier enthusiasm for intensive fieldwork has waned over the years. Assuming that even as Neendakara deliveries shift further from home to hospital, the share of mission hospitals remains substantial, a question then would arise with respect to its impact on the acceptance of family planning in the village. Will acceptance of family planning be therefore less among the fisherfolk of Neendakara than among the fisherfolk of Sakthikulangara, though both belong to the same Christian denomination? It is difficult to answer the question. However, it is still possible that family planning acceptance in Neendakara may not fall far behind Sakthikulangara judging from the noticeably greater increase in the mean age at marriage of women in Neendakara than in Sakthikulangara during the current century.

Table III.20   Distribution of births in Neendakara by place of delivery and type of institution, 1950–1979

			Public Hospital		Private Hospital	
Period	Home	Hospital	Govt hospital	Foundation hospital	Mission hospital	Private hospital
1950–54	96.3	3.7	2.5	–	1.2	–
1955–59	99.3	0.7	0.7	–	–	–
1960–64	99.7	0.3	0.3	–	–	–
1965–69	97.4	2.6	1.5	0.8	1.0	–
1970–74	61.5	38.5	6.0	0.8	22.8	1.5
1975–79	50.7	49.3	10.2	0.4	35.8	2.8

Source: St. Sebastian Church, Parish Records.

Age at marriage

Table III.21 gives the mean age at first marriage for both men and women in Neendakara Parish from 1901 to 1979. It can be seen that the mean age at marriage of men and women during 1901–10 was almost the same as in Sakthikulangara for both men and women. During 1971–79, Neendakara's mean age at marriage was 26.36 for men and 19.67 for women as against Sakthikulangara's 25.31 and 17.71 respectively. The gap is particularly noticeable with respect to women's age at marriage.

Looking ahead

It is interesting that two groups of fisherfolk, which not only are geographically and culturally so very close to each other but also have been undergoing a process of very close economic integration over the past twenty years, still can show some quite divergent trends with respect to factors which can have an impact on demographic developments.

Table III.21   Mean age at first marriage in Neendakara Parish, 1901–1979

Year	Male age at marriage	Female age at marriage
1901–10	24.03	16.19
1911–20	24.32	16.28
1921–30	25.05	17.05
1931–40	27.44	19.98
1941–50	26.28	18.91
1951–60	27.95	20.14
1961–70	25.43	18.88
1971–79	26.36	19.67

Source: St. Sebastian Church, Parish Records.

D.   Puthenthura Village

The same National Highway that runs through Sakthikulangara and Neendakara connects them to Puthenthura which is not more than three kilometres north of Neendakara Bridge. Being on the highway, many public buses pass through Puthenthura. Several of them make a stop here, but to get in depends on whether there is room. There is also a half hourly bus service, which costs 40 paise (approximately US $0.05) to commute to or from Sakthikulangara. Lately, private mini-buses have started operating in the region. They are much more expensive, however. From Puthenthura to Sakthikulangara or back, a mini-bus would charge one rupee, i.e., two and a half times what a public bus charges. Most people, men as well as women, commute to and from Sakthikulangara on foot. Even when they have to go long distances they walk up to Sakthikulangara because it is easier to get into a bus there.

The highway cuts through the village, dividing it into two halves. On the west is a stretch of sandy land lying between the sea and the highway. It is here that one sees the cluster of huts, close to four hundred in number, which comprise the principal part of the village. Unlike most non-fishing villages, a fishing village in Kerala, regardless of its religious composition, tends to be of the cluster type. East of the highway is land interlaced with backwaters. While on the west side there is hardly any vegetation, the east side is refreshingly green with its palms, vegetation and backwaters. Here there are a hundred houses put up by the government as part of its programme for providing improved housing to the economically backward groups in the state.

The Foundation hospital

Going north from Neendakara Bridge, a major landmark that one cannot miss before reaching Puthenthura is what is commonly referred to as the Foundation hospital. Its formal name is the Indo-Norwegian Medical College Health Unit. The unit was put up under the Norwegian Aid Programme to serve the total population of the Project area.

When the health unit was started, the major emphasis was preventive medicine and improvement in the health of mothers and young children. A clinic for mothers and children was put up in 1954 and a maternity ward with 16 beds was added within a year. It was also in 1955 that a sub-centre of the health unit was opened at Sakthikulangara and a tuberculosis outpatient clinic was added to the main centre. The latter clinic was provided with an X-ray screening unit in 1957. As the demand rose from the public for curative facilities, two curative clinics were also started in 1957. A separate children's ward, with 24 beds, was set up in 1962. In 1963 the management of the whole health unit, including its sub-centre, was handed over to the state government. To start with, the unit was administered by the State Department of Health Services but in 1966 it was handed to the Government Medical College in Trivandrum. Now, the unit functions also as a health training centre for medical and paramedical personnel, and is administered by the Department of Social and Preventive Medicine of the College. The centre has six clinics, including leprosy and dental clinics which were started in 1967 and 1969, respectively, in addition to the maternity and children's wards with 16 and 24 beds respectively. Originally, the services of the centre were open to only people from the Project area, but after its administration passed into the hands of the college, the services were extended to the neighbouring villages.

Family planning

Though no new beds have been added to the maternity ward since it was started in 1955 with 16 beds, the number of deliveries handled has been increasing rather rapidly. Between 1961 and 1972, the increase registered in this regard was five-fold. Post-partum sterilisations were also undertaken here, but it took people some years to accept them. From the available evaluation reports on the working of the whole health unit, it would appear that one of the main obstacles to the acceptance of post-partum sterilisation was anaesthesia. People found it painful and complained of severe, frequent backaches and headaches during follow-up. Initiative was taken by the doctors of the health unit to perform post-partum sterilisation under local anaesthesia and this improved the acceptance of sterilisation considerably. Thus while in 1968 the percentage of post-partum sterilisations to hospital deliveries was 9.4, it went up to 54.9 in 1972. Although vasectomy operations were also started in 1964, their acceptance in the community has been rather nominal.

The health reports indicate that the overall response to the medical facilities offered by the health centre was very positive right from the very beginning, and that the facilities of the maternity ward were soon over-extended. In fact, the most recent available data indicate that admission was provided for as many as sixty patients as against the bed capacity of only sixteen. There can be little doubt, therefore, that the health unit has not only provided invaluable service to the people of the Project area but also helped in the popularisation of family planning. Still, people of the area complain generally of a deterioration in the attention and service they receive at the health unit now, compared to what it offered in its early phase. To some extent, the deterioration in service may have been the direct result of the decision to extend the services of the unit beyond the Project area without at the same time expanding the unit's capacity. However, anyone now visiting the unit cannot but notice not only the congestion but also the poor state of the unit's equipment, buildings and environment.

Near the health unit are a few brick buildings which house an exporting firm, an ice factory and a bank. These buildings are also on the western side of the highway. It is after these that one comes to the main settlement of the fishing households. At the very entrance to the settlement, one sees a dilapidated building which at one time housed the local office of the Araya Seva Samithi, the service organisation of the Hindu fishermen all over Kerala, but is now in virtual disuse.

The Araya fishermen

The Hindu fishermen of Kerala State belong to one of the three fishing castes. There are the Arayas, the Mukkuvans and the Valans. Though the traditional occupation of these three castes is fishing, there is no inter-marriage between the people of these castes. The Arayas of different villages have organised themselves into Araya Karayogams (*karayogam* means association of hamlets) which together make Araya Seva Samithi at the state level. Indeed at the state level, all the Hindu fishing castes have joined into a federal body called Akhila Kerala Dheevara Sabha, an organisation which aims at safeguarding the social, economic and political interests of these castes.

The Araya Seva Samithi

Over 90 per cent of the fishing population of Puthenthura belongs to the Araya caste. All the Araya households of the village are members of the local *karayogam* and therefore come under the discipline of the Samithi. The *karayogam* was founded in Puthenthura in 1943. A Committee was set up consisting of a president, secretary-treasurer and six other members. They are elected every two years on the basis of one vote for each adult. Each member household pays a monthly subscription of one rupee to meet the Committee's expenses. The Committee settles disputes between members, registers marriages, records dowries, mediates in marital disputes and organises religious and social festivities. While there is no legal sanction behind the Committee's decisions, the general support of members gives its decisions a strong backing, and individual members do not ordinarily violate these decisions for fear of general disapproval. Thus the Committee can be said to perform several functions which the church performs in the other two villages where Latin Catholics predominate.

The west-side settlement

At the back of the abandoned building of the Araya Seva Samithi is another brick building which houses a village post office and reading room. From that point on, westward and northward, are huddled together in a seemingly random fashion some 300 huts of fishing households. The huts, without exception, are made entirely of thatch, the only difference between huts being of size or age or both. The thatch used for walls has to be replaced every five years and that used for the roof every three years. But not all households can do this on time. The Government Upper Primary School housed in a brick building marks, more or less, the northern boundary of this settlement, sandwiched on the narrow strip of land between the coast on the west and the highway on the east. The whole terrain is bare with virtually no palms or other trees to provide some shelter from the midday sun when it gets unbearably hot in summer. Part of the reason why the whole place is so bare could be that all land here is public property, which may be taken away from the people living on it. The area is considered rich in ilmenite and the state government keeps coming out with plans to exploit it. Luckily for these people, these plans have been taking time to get translated into action.

The east-side settlement

On the eastern side of the highway is the temple which is one of the main landmarks here. Then there are a few shops and as one proceeds north, one comes to the dispensary of the Employees' State Insurance Hospital. The services of this dispensary are available only to employees of such factories and other establishments within a specified jurisdiction which are members of the employees' state insurance scheme managed by the central government. The village folk have no access to the dispensary. The hundred brick houses which the government built some time back for the fishermen here cannot easily be seen from the highway. The houses are laid out in rows with proper access roads, street lights and access to protected water taps. The people have planted palms and other trees in their individual plots. The more enterprising ones do some gardening as well. Access to water is no problem because of the small river next door, and water taps located at convenient points. The houses are of the same size, unlike the huts on the west side. Each house has a built area of 300 square feet and some open space around it. Each house is made of baked bricks and cement plaster and has a tiled roof. People living in these houses were originally living on the west side and practically every one here has a relation or two living there.

The fish landing site

The site for the traditional craft to land is to the rear of the west-side settlement. A couple of huts close to the site have opened tea shops for use by the village fishermen. The number of tea shops increases and decreases depending on the seasonal fluctuations of the fish catch. Also, there are a few thatched sheds put up collectively for use when it is too hot under the sun.

Notwithstanding all that has happened in the Project area since the Project was launched in 1953, Puthenthura is still a traditional fishing village, judging by the technology used in the village for fishing. The two types of crafts used here are the *thanguvallom,* carrying a crew of nine to eleven persons, and the *kochuvallom,* carrying a crew of four to five persons. Some efforts are being made currently to persuade fishermen here to have their craft fitted with outboard engines. Easy finance is provided by the manufacturing firms directly or indirectly. But this is still in an experimental stage. Only five crafts have so far been equipped with outboard engines.

It was in Puthenthura that the attempt to introduce mechanised boats was first made under the Norwegian Aid Programme. Initially, however, the acceptance was not very satisfactory. The reasons probably were many, but the most important one was the very low horse power of the first mechanised boats. The boats, 20 to 22 feet in length, were fitted with engines of eight to ten horse power and were meant for four or five fishermen. Being heavier than the local craft, these boats needed more men for landing and launching than the crew itself. The boats fished for the same sardines and mackerels found close to the shore as the local craft. Thus while the mechanised crafts did not show any significant advantage over the traditional craft in range, they were found to be twice as expensive as the traditional craft in terms of operating costs alone. Maintenance also was very much more expensive and more time consuming. Though the boats were sold at 50 per cent of the cost price and became the property of the fishermen, the capital cost still worked out to be very much higher in comparison to the non-subsidised cost of the comparable local craft. So, the economics of the boats first introduced were not quite convincing. There probably were a host of other factors which confused the economics of the technological change, at least initially. The use of ice had not been introduced. On days of bumper catch, prices would crash and fish would have to be either sold at rock bottom price or allowed to rot. Also, possibly the chain of communication of the Project personnel with the fishermen took time to take roots. The fact that Puthenthura village did not have a protected landing site of its own where boats could conveniently be berthed may also have been a dampening factor. Anyway the net result was that Puthenthura took to mechanised boats rather marginally as compared to Neendakara and Sakthikulangara. Thus today, only eight out of 419 mechanised boats owned in the Project area belong to the fishing households from Puthenthura. Of course, as has been indicated earlier in this chapter, the proportion of fishermen engaged in mechanised fishing is not so low. This has come about with increasing involvement, over the years, of men from the fishing households of Puthenthura in various jobs on mechanised boats. Direct benefits of the Project have, therefore, accrued to Puthenthura mostly through the services provided by the Foundation hospital and generation of some new jobs for the local people in the pipe factory located to the north of Puthenthura.

So, even today the fishing crafts are, like elsewhere along the Kerala coast, powered by oars and launched from and landed on the coast every day during the various fishing seasons. The coast of Puthenthura enjoys no natural protection. While the craft can land their catches all along the coast, they concentrate within a stretch of about 500 yards, considered the least unsafe by the fishermen. The activity on the landing site is in the mornings and afternoons. During peak periods, when the catch is expected to be good, you find not only cyclists but also trucks from far and near coming to Puthenthura to transport fish to the interior. A few elderly women headload fish vendors, who can be counted on one's finger tips, are there practically on all days when local crafts go out to sea.

They all buy fish by auction conducted right after a craft lands its catch. While women fish vendors carry their wares on foot to distances within 10 kilometres, cyclist vendors, who generally dominate auction purchases at the Puthenthura landing centre, carry fish longer distances, and the trucks still longer distances. All of them, including women fish vendors, now use ice which is available from the nearby ice factory. The proceeds of every catch are shared between the owner of a craft and the crew. For *thanguvallom,* the owner's share is one-third, and for *kochuvallom,* the owner's share is two-fifths. The rest is distributed equally between the crew.

Age at marriage

Although, as was stated above, the local committee of the Araya Seva Samithi performs some of the functions that the church performs among the fisherfolk of Neendakara and Sakthikulangara, the records kept in Puthenthura do not lend themselves to the same sort of analysis as the church records. To obtain a comparative picture with respect to some important demographic aspects, information for all three villages was collected on the basis of cluster sampling with respect to age at marriage, number of pregnancies and acceptance of family planning for over 250 couples in each of the three villages.

Table III.22 shows that though the age at marriage of women in Puthenthura was already quite high in 1931–40, it still has kept rising. In the decade 1971–80 the female age at marriage had come close to 20. In Sakthikulangara and Neendakara the corresponding figures work out to 18.6 and 18.7 respectively on the basis of the data collected in the manner explained above.

Table III.22   Mean female age at marriage in Project villages, 1931–80

Period	Puthen-thura	Sakthi-kulangara	Neenda-kara
1931–1940	18.3	17.3	17.9
1941–1950	18.6	17.9	17.8
1951–1960	18.0	17.8	18.4
1961–1970	18.9	17.7	18.8
1971–1980	19.8	18.6	18.7

Source: Data collected for this study.

Pregnancies per married woman

The data on live pregnancies occurring to married women are tabulated separately for each of the three Project villages in Table III.23. It can be seen that the average number of pregnancies occurring to women of all ages works out to be the lowest for Puthenthura, but also for women up to age 60 and for women up to age 40. At the same time, it is clear that the number of pregnancies per married woman has been on the decline for all three villages. Interestingly, however, it appears that in Puthenthura the rate of this decline was already quite steep in the generation before that of the married women who are currently 40 years of age. On the other hand, in Sakthikulangara and Neendakara, it is this generation which is experiencing a steep decline in the number of pregnancies.

Table III.23   Average number of live pregnancies per married woman in
              Project villages

Age group	Sakthi-kulangara	Neenda-kara	Puthen-thura
To married women of all ages	4.74	3.86	3.70
To married women of up to 60 years	4.19	3.69	2.28
To married women up to 40 years	2.95	2.60	2.07
Number of couples for which information was collected	262	250	251

Source: Data collected for this study, 1980.

Acceptance of family planning

To complement the information with respect to pregnancies occurring to married women, it was possible to gather information with respect to the acceptance of family planning by married women still in the reproductive group and those who have crossed the threshold recently. It ought to be made clear that acceptance of family planning in these villages amounts to acceptance of sterilisation.

It can be seen from Table III.24 that acceptance of family planning is close to 50 per cent in all three villages and that Puthenthura is somewhat ahead of Neendakara in this regard. It still remains unexplained though that with around the same level of acceptance of family planning in the three villages, Puthenthura manages to keep the average number of pregnancies distinctly lower than that in both Sakthikulangara and Neendakara.

59

Table III.24 Acceptance of family planning in Project villages

Age group	Sakthi-kulangara	Neenda-kara	Puthen-thura
1. Total number of married women aged 40 or below in the sample	130	177	141
2. Total number of married women aged 40 or below accepting family planning in the sample	76 (58.5%)	89 (50.3%)	75 (53.2%)
3. Total number of married women aged 50 or below in the sample	161	209	181
4. Total number of married women aged 50 or below accepting family planning in the sample	86 (53.4%)	96 (45.9%)	92 (50.8%)

Source: Data collected for this study, 1980.

Summary of Observations

In this brief summary of the main findings of our study so far we briefly highlight the main changes — technological, economic and demographic — that have occurred in the Project area over nearly three decades after the first attempt was made to introduce modern technologies of fishing and fish preservation.

Technological change

1. On the basis of the information available at the macro level, the impact of technological change in terms of mechanised fishing and the adoption of modern methods of fish preservation has been enormous in the three study villages.

2. The extent of the technological change however has been quite unequal in the three villages. The maximum impact has been on Sakthikulangara, the village closest to the main boat jetty. It is somewhat less in Neendakara, the other Latin Catholic village across the highway bridge from the main jetty, and the least in the Araya Hindu village, Puthenthura, which is located some distance away from the main boat jetty.

3. Over the years, there has been a steady increase in the number of mechanised boats owned by fishermen and a decrease in the number of traditional crafts,

particularly in the two Latin Catholic villages. In 1980 there were 419 mechanised fishing boats as against none in 1953 and 187 traditional crafts in 1980 as against 477 in 1953.

4. The use of ice for preservation seems to have taken firm root and spread uniformly in all three villages irrespective of the method of fishing employed. Even women headload fish vendors use ice when they store their fish or take it out to sell.

5. There has been a significant increase in the infrastructure facilities in terms of production of ice and the establishment of freezing and cold storage capacity. In 1980 there were 29 ice plants with a production capacity of 377 tonnes and storage capacity of 325 tonnes. Also there were 15 freezing plants with a frozen storage capacity of 1,625 tonnes. There existed nothing of the sort in 1953.

Economic change

6. Since the technological change was followed closely by the discovery of major new prawn grounds, a distinct improvement has taken place in the opportunities for employment and income generation in the area comprising the aforesaid three villages and their neighbourhood.

7. There has been a phenomenal increase in the total catch landings of fish and prawns in the area. Not only is the composition of the catch very different now but also the shift has been altogether towards higher value varieties. The catch which was in the neighbourhood of only 2,000 tons in 1953 rose to about 85,000 tons in 1980. Over two-fifths of the quantity now caught are high value exportable varieties like prawns, squids and lobsters. Though the value of the prawn catch has been fluctuating violently, it has not affected the incomes of the fishermen as the unit value realised has been consistently increasing.

8. The overemphasis on prawn fishing has, however, introduced profound seasonality in fishing operations, with the concentration of activity during the three monsoon months between June and September. In 1980, the catch in the three months of July, August and September accounted for two-thirds of the annual total. The area is now exposed to mechanised boats from the neighbouring districts during these busy months leading to tremendous congestion and unhygienic conditions particularly in places of public use such as the landing jetty, parking lot and village lanes. More than 2,000 mechanised trawlers operate in the area during the peak season.

9. The export from the area of marine products has increased enormously. In 1953, only dried prawns and fish valued at less than Rs. 100,000 were exported to nearby countries like Sri Lanka and Burma. In 1979–80, marine products exported were valued at Rs. 92.18 million.

10. Mechanised fishing is now the dominant source of income and employment in

the two Latin Catholic villages of the study area. Most of the menfolk in these villages either own mechanised boats or work for them. Even in households still operating in the traditional sector, there is usually at least one member working in the mechanised sector of fishing. This of course applies to the two Latin Catholic villages which have accepted the shift to mechanisation and not to the Hindu Araya village where its acceptance has been rather marginal. That being the position, mechanisation has increased the disparities in income not only within the villages but also between the villages. Improvement in incomes as well as the increase in disparities is clearly visible in the housing in the area.

11. New work opportunities have opened up for fisherwomen in the trading and processing of marine products ·and net making. These work opportunities are in general better paying than the opportunities for work that existed prior to mechanisation.

12. Participation by women in new work opportunities is widespread in all three villages so that work participation by women has distinctly improved over time.

13. There is also a distinct change in the civil condition of the women workers of these villages. Earlier, either widowed, aged or divorced women or unmarried girls from single parent households took paid work. Now, married women and unmarried girls from two-parent households account for the large majority of working women from all three villages. Thus, women's work participation has improved qualitatively as well as quantitatively in not only the Latin Catholic villages which accepted mechanisation of fishing but also the Araya Hindu village which did not quite accept mechanisation. Qualitatively, however, the women from the Latin Catholic villages still have an edge because of their easier access to better paying work opportunities.

Demographic changes

14. There is a marked improvement in the sex ratio in favour of women in all three Project villages indicating a lowering of both female infant and maternal mortality rates.

15. The proportion of births with institutional help has increased significantly in all three villages. While in Sakthikulangara and Puthenthura nearly 100 per cent of the births take place under institutional care, in Neendakara more than 50 per cent of the births are conducted in hospitals or nursing homes. Even this lower proportion for Neendakara is not lower than the proportion of births taking place under institutional care for the rural areas of the state as a whole which stood at 36 per cent in 1977. Even for the country as a whole, institutionalised birth stood at only 17 per cent for the rural areas and 35 per cent for the urban areas.

16. The average number of live pregnancies for married women below 40 years of age has come down considerably in all three villages. In the Araya Hindu Villages, this decline has been quite steep.

17. The acceptance of family planning is close to 50 per cent in all three villages, regardless of religion. At the same time female sterilisation is the only accepted form for limiting the family size.

Overall changes

Reviewing the overall changes that have occurred in the three Project villages in these past 25 years we can see certain major differences. One thing that is very clear is that the impact of mechanisation has been very different in all three villages. It has been of greater intensity in Sakthikulangara, the village nearest to the public boat jetty. It would almost appear that the order of change has been less as one moves away from the public boat jetty, which became the centre of activity for mechanised fishing. At the same time we cannot overlook the changes which have come about in the other two villages.

Sakthikulangara has marched ahead in regard to the ownership of boats. At the same time, however, going by the distribution of boat ownership, the economic inequalities in Sakthikulangara are possibly greater now among the fishermen there than in Neendakara and Puthenthura.

The contrasts within the village in housing are quite sharp and can be noticed even by a casual observer. Maximum income increases have been experienced by owners of mechanised boats, and this has caused and continues to cause intra-village and inter-village tensions. Precisely because a major part of the activity connected with mechanised fishing is concentrated in Sakthikulangara it has led to considerable congestion and consequent general deterioration of hygiene in the village. With so many people converging on the public jetty without proper civic and other amenities, severe problems of pollution have been created. Neendakara is by comparison much less polluted and Puthenthura, of course, even less.

Neendakara and Puthenthura have not altogether been bypassed by the technological change in fishing. This can be seen easily from the involvement not only of fishermen of these two villages in activities connected with mechanised fishing but also of fisherwomen. So economic prosperity cannot be said to be altogether confined only to the village of Sakthikulangara. Indeed, people from other neighbouring villages have also benefited from the increased economic activity generated in the Project area as a result of the resort to mechanised fishing.

Not only are many more women occupied in income-generating activities there than ever before but also the type of these activities is different and somewhat better. The new work opportunities are less demanding physically and offer a little more income, even when the women continue to be subject to no less exploitative relationships. If one notices today greater use of medical facilities, both private and public, it is possibly due not only to the establishment of hospitals, public and private, but also to the increased awareness of their usefulness as a result of the expansion of education, particularly among the women of fishing households. But the trend towards higher female age at marriage and smaller family size in all three villages may be the combined result of the spread of education, increased involvement in work by women and greater access to medical facilities.

In the next chapter we look in detail at the lives of 10 women.

CHAPTER IV

PROFILES OF WOMEN

Sakthikulangara
Case Study – A

MAGGIE

The headload fish vendor

Name	MAGGIE	No. of children lost under 5 years of age	One
Village	Sakthikulangara		
Age	36	Family planning status	Operated after eight children
Education	Nil	Occupation	Fish vending in houses and prawn trading
Age at marriage	15		
Dowry	Rs. 300	Husband's occupation	Coolie fisherman, and later craft owner
No. of pregnancies	Eight	Ownership status	Owns a house and a small traditional craft
No. of births in hospital	Five		
No. of births at home	Two	Type of house	Hut

I was born and brought up in Sakthikulangara very near the present boat jetty. In those days, when I was a child, we could just walk over to the bay. Now, the place has changed beyond recognition with sheds and factories lined up all along.

Our hut was so close to the sea-shore that we were always scared of its being washed away. The area was exposed to intense erosion and very often palms and huts would get washed away in the monsoon season. However for us, its location was very convenient as my grandmother worked for a big house close by as a maid servant. The family she worked for was a leading family of this village, in terms of not only wealth, but also education.

Family background

My grandmother was raised in this family's house as a child. She must have started helping in the kitchen from the age of 5 or 6. Though she never got married, she had three children, one boy and two girls, who grew up in that very house. My father

65

Janice was one of these three children. Even to this day we never have asked our mother about the family background of my father; we knew it was some thing we could not be very proud of.

My mother really grew up in Quilon city, some 10 kilometres south of Sakthikulangara. Her parents lived by street singing. At one time a whole community of street singers lived behind the Quilon Railway Station. My mother's parents would come occasionally to the two Christian fishing villages to sing on special occasions. That is how they came to know my father's mother. My parents were married in a simple ceremony in the church with no dowry. After his marriage my father put up a thatched hut at a little distance from the big house where my grandmother worked.

My brothers and sisters

My parents had seven children. Of these two died as infants. All the children were delivered by mother in the hut. My mother had been married only for 14 years when first my 13-year old brother and then my father died in a cholera epidemic in quick succession. My mother became a widow at 36 with four children to raise. She was illiterate and had acquired no special skills. Before her marriage she had known street singing and after marriage she was raising her family with a child born to her practically every two years. She did manage to do some part-time work as a water carrier. This meant carting water to the houses that needed drinking water from the wells and she would be paid for this service. Water was a very scarce resource in those days and we had to commute long distances to cart water. It was virtually rationed in the households and most of our quarrels centered around it in the family. This was an important source of employment to many women.

Trip to Singapore

When I was around ten years old the people with whom my father's mother worked were looking for a young girl to go with their son and his family to Singapore for four years on a teaching assignment. I was chosen as a domestic help on my grandmother's recommendation. I remember the long sea journey and how I got sick. I did not eat for days on end until we reached Kuala Lumpur. Looking back, I enjoyed my stay in Singapore. They looked after me very well. I had to help them with their three little children. During my four-year stay in Singapore, my food and clothing were entirely taken care of. Also, I was given some pocket money.

Our contact with other nationalities was minimal; we were more or less confined to socialising with people from Kerala. I did meet some Malayalee young men but the question of my marrying one of them did not arise. I was to come back with the family after four years.

The first marriage

Within a year of my return from Singapore my marriage was arranged. There was a woman water carrier, a Syrian Christian, who had migrated from Ernakulam to

Quilon, by the name of Eliyamma, a local derivative for Elizabeth. How a Syrian Christian woman came to live among Latin Christian fishermen has remained a mystery. She worked first for the Austin family, which has always been prominent in politics. Later on, she got a job in the local church school on their recommendation. Though I had met her son, Yohannan, even before I went to Singapore, I had no idea that I had made any impact on him. Apparently he had made up his mind and let it be known that he would wait for my return. At the age of fifteen, I was married to Yohannan who was twenty-four. It was a church wedding and we were married at the St. Britto's Church. A sum of Rs. 300 was handed over to Eliyamma as dowry by my former employers.

Once married, I moved to Eliyamma's house to live with Yohannan. I must have given birth to our first child within one year. It was delivered at home. It lived only for sixteen days. When I was expecting my second child, Eliyamma took me to the government hospital in Quilon. I delivered a boy. He was baptised as Antony.

I become a widow

When our son was hardly six months old, Yohannan died in an accident at sea. While the other crew members swam to the shore, Yohannan could not, as he was not a good swimmer. Eliyamma and I lost our sole male support with an added responsibility of an infant to look after. Eliyamma was kind enough to ask me to continue to stay with her. She saw in her six-month old grandson her sole consolation and drive to live. I stayed home for about a year. Then I took to fish vending, the only job I could possibly do. Eliyamma would take care of the child when I was out vending fish.

My second marriage

While Eliyamma supported me and my son with an open heart, she was keen that I must think in terms of remarriage. It was she who found a second match for me. Xavier was an orphan boy who had been adopted by a family in the village on the other side of the creek. He was 25 years old then and had been working as a coolie fisherman for some years. But he had never been to school.

Eliyamma offered to give the 300 rupees dowry which I had brought in at the time of my marriage to Yohannan. If a girl becomes a widow at a young age, the dowry money must be returned so that she can remarry.

To start with, I moved to Xavier's foster home. Eliyamma offered to keep my toddler son with her. But we did not stay in Neendakara for more than a few months. I missed my son and also Eliyamma. Moreover, I felt that I was an added burden on Xavier's foster family. Once I could persuade Xavier to move with me back to Sakthikulangara, we lost no time. Eliyamma welcomed us with open arms and allowed us to stay in her hut. I delivered my first child from Xavier, Sosha, a girl, in Eliyamma's hut.

Undergoing sterilisation

The reason I did not go to the hospital for my delivery was that I was taken by surprise by pains and there was little time for me to be removed to the hospital. After that, I had five more children, four sons and one daughter. They were all delivered at the Project hospital. I had no problem with any delivery, but during my fifth and sixth pregnancies I was asked several times if I would have them terminated. "Haven't you had enough? Why don't you people concentrate on the ones you have already?" These were the questions I heard often when I went to the hospital. Somehow the idea was frightening. I did not even discuss it with Xavier or anyone else. After my sixth child the doctors told me that it was time for me to go in for sterilisation but both Xavier and Eliyamma, on whom I depended for all advice and help, were reluctant. Still, I could somehow bring them around. Neither of them wanted me to have more children, but they were worried that there might be post-operation complications. I had had my first child when I was only 16 and since then I had been doing little other than delivering and feeding babies and also working. I am really happy that I do not have to bear any more children thanks to the operation. But it has left me weak and I get, as a result, severe headaches and backaches once in a while but there are no other complications. The doctors feel I am imagining and it is due to my age and general weakness. I am not sure whether they are telling me the truth or just consoling me.

Our separate hut

Soon after the birth of Sosha, my first child from my second marriage, we put up a separate hut on a piece of land Eliyamma had bought recently near to the plot on which her own house was built. That is when Xavier and I moved along with little Sosha to our house, and Antony stayed behind with Eliyamma. Since we continued to stay in the same compound, I never really felt separated from my son. It is in this hut that I brought up Sosha and the other five children, altogether four boys and two girls, from my second marriage.

Our hut

Our hut is of very modest proportions. Within a total built area of 16 feet by 13 feet, we have three small rooms and a long verandah. The long narrow wooden table is in the verandah along with a bench. Menfolk have their lunch and dinner on this table. But the verandah serves also as our living room. I have kept three wrought-iron chairs, with back and seat woven with plastic cane, for use by our visitors. The photographs you see above the two doors on the whitewashed brick wall are mostly of my children and grandchildren. Pictures of Eliyamma taken at the school she was working for are in the most prominent place. The clothes-lines running across the whole verandah is to keep one's work clothes for the night. We don't have any cupboards to fold and keep our clothes, men's or women's. These clothes-lines, strings tied from one wall to the other, are our cupboards.

My child from the first marriage

Antony is my first son, as you know, by my first marriage to Yohannan. He was with me only for three years, even less. After I got remarried, he stayed with his grandmother, Eliyamma, even though I saw him practically every day. He has virtually been raised by her. He went to the same school where Eliyamma was the water carrier, and studied until the tenth standard, but never got through the final examination. Now, Antony is 27 years old, married to the daughter of an owner of a mechanised boat. He runs a chit fund on a modest scale. It has been formally registered. As such, its operations are subject to certain public restrictions through special legislation. It is really a savings club and in Sakthikulangara these days, they exist in all sizes. From the very beginning, Eliyamma did not want him to have anything to do with fishing. All the lump sum amount she got on her retirement from school service and what Antony got in cash by way of dowry at the time of his marriage have been invested in this chit fund business. With experience he has started doing reasonably well. More and more people come to him to keep their extra cash. But he still has to go around to collect the contributions as they fall due, to keep the defaults as small as possible. On that, in fact, depends the success of this business.

Eliyamma, Antony, his wife and their 1-year old son live in a large house made of baked bricks and cement concrete roofing. On their 15 *cents* of land they have put up two identical houses. They live in one house and have rented the second house which is in front and close to the road to a doctor who runs a clinic. He gets a rent of Rs. 100. Both houses have electric connection and proper bath and toilets. But they still have to rely on the well as there is no proper water connection. They have dug a well in their own compound.

Antony is of immense help to me and my family. Xavier and I and my grown-up sons are all members of one or the other of his chit funds. When we are in need of funds, he is always willing to help us.

My daughter Sosha

Sosha, the elder of my two daughters, is now 25 years old, married, with two children, a daughter and a son. I kept Sosha at school only for four years. When she was ten years old she started helping me with not only housekeeping chores and child-care but also with my work. She would peel the prawns I brought home in the evenings. This was a help as the export companies accept prawns only in peeled form during certain specified hours. I got Sosha married when she was only fifteen because we got such a good match for her. The boy was ten years older than her, but he was a well educated young man, a trained welder and already making a decent living. He has been in school for some ten years and is a handsome young man. His father, though from a far off-fishing village, has been virtually living in Sakthikulangara with his daughter. We agreed to give Rs. 2,500 in cash as dowry and 60 grams of gold worth Rs. 1,200. All told, it meant an expenditure of Rs. 5,000. The decision to get Sosha married was a collective one of Xavier, Eliyamma and myself, though I was the one who pursued the matter most actively. We pooled money for the dowry from various sources. Eliyamma lent us some, and some we had to borrow from neighbours and friends. Also, Xavier and I had some savings in our chit funds. Sosha's husband used the dowry money, including the cash he could raise by pawning the jewellery to go to the Gulf. He has been working there for the last four years.

My children from the second marriage

Titus, my second child from my marriage with Xavier, is some $2\frac{1}{2}$ years younger than Sosha. He studied until the seventh standard and started working thereafter with his father on the traditional craft. He tried to work for mechanised crafts, but that makes him sick. He cannot stand the diesel smell and the vibrations. Sosha's husband has arranged for the immigration clearance which means getting a no-objection certificate, popularly known as a NOC. He will go and work for a local contractor in Kuwait as an unskilled labourer. We have spent almost Rs. 15,000 in all on the NOC, his air ticket and his clothes. Antony has been a great help in raising the local funds. Sosha's husband will be paid back directly by Titus once he starts earning in Kuwait. Titus is my good son. He does not smoke or drink. He brought back home all the money he earned as a fisherman. So I have no doubt that he will not only repay all the money we borrowed for him but also help us with whatever additional funds we need for settling our other children and constructing a better house for ourselves.

Eighteen-year old Joseph stayed in school to complete the ninth standard. He is now a full-time fisherman, going with Titus on our *kochuvallom,* the small traditional craft. With Titus gone to the Gulf, he will be needed more by his father. But I would like him to start working for a mechanised craft where the earnings are much higher, although seasonal. Even if he too wants to go with his brother to the Gulf, I would be happy; we will be able to save in a short while the money needed for his NOC and air ticket.

The second daughter's affairs

Mariamma, our second daughter, was studying in the eighth standard when she had an affair with a neighbour's son. Since she was expecting, we had to save the situation by somehow getting the two married before people came to know about the affair. She was three years under age however. With the new legislation, the church would not allow any girl to marry before eighteen. We had to put great pressure on the parish priest to get her married. The boy has been at school only for four years. He has not settled down to proper work, not even as a fisherman. None of us is happy about the choice. We would have mobilised enough funds to get her married well. Now it is no use; Mariamma is already expecting her first child.

The last two

My last two sons, Jose 13, and Joy 11, are still in school. Jose is in the seventh standard and Joy in the fourth standard. If they show sufficient interest in studies, I shall have no objection to their completing school. In fact we all would very much like them to go in for some technical training thereafter so that they too can go to the Gulf, if it is still possible to do so. For a good living here, they would probably need such training even more. Moreover, we can afford to have them in school longer. I would have liked even Mariamma to complete her school but her lucky stars evidently were not in the right position.

My daily routine

I get up quite early, at about six o'clock in the morning. I go to the bushes and then to watch out for the incoming country crafts. I carry my basket with me. Other female fish vendors of this village, most of them in their late forties, also come to the sea-shore. The landing centre for country crafts is close to the old lighthouse, which stands as a silent monument to the old days. All the crafts including Xavier's are berthed on sand. During rough weather, they are pulled inland. I buy fish for vending from any craft. Apart from the fact that the time when Xavier comes back with his catch may not always suit me most, it makes little difference from whom I buy my fish. Even Xavier's fish catch must go through auction, for often he has to share the proceeds with one or two persons from outside of our own family who work as crew members. Actually, if both the boys went out with Xavier, then they would not need any outsider. But I am always scared to send all three out to sea in one boat. If there is an accident we would lose all of them.

After buying fish I walk back home. Sosha by then has cleaned the house and cooked breakfast. Very rarely do we depend on the leftover rice and rice gruel of the previous night any more. Those days are luckily left behind us. We cook fresh breakfast every day. After breakfast I go fish vending with the basket on my head. I go to the houses of my regular customers in Marathadi, a locality within Sakthikulangara where the Hindu population is residing. There are also a few tea shops who buy fish from me for their daily requirement.

I sell mostly on a cash basis but there will always be some who cannot immediately pay me either in part or in full. Usually they pay up the next day or the day after that. Often they ask me if I will go back later in the day to collect money. So I go back to them after disposing of the leftover fish in a wayside market. If the quantity I have to dispose of is large, I go to the main market where there is a section for women fish vendors. We all squat on the floor with our baskets placed in front. On my way back home, I stop at a tea shop for a cup of tea. But I take my midday meal at home with Sosha, who does the major part of the housekeeping including cooking in our house. After our midday meal, I help Sosha with the cleaning of vessels before lying down for about half an hour. Lunch consists of rice and fish curry and rarely tapioca. Men do eat at home, i.e., lunch and dinner. Sosha and I have lunch only after the men have eaten. They eat on the long bench on the verandah and we eat in the kitchen itself. There is enough food for all so we do not make any difference in the distribution of food between girls and boys. Children take fried fish, chutney and rice to school. This is considered clean food as it does not drip and is easy to handle.

I get ready to reach the jetty by about three in the afternoon. I have been going there for the last four years. At the jetty I participate in the auctions of shrimp catch. As a mechanised craft lands its catch, the auction is organised immediately for each basket. The auction agents are all men and the bidders cluster around the basket. If the basket contains expensive prawns, mostly men bidders bid for it. If it contains a mixed assortment then women compete with each other for it. I sell to the representatives and agents of exporting firms who do not have the time and energy to watch out for every boat and participate in the auction. I often stay on at the jetty till about 6:30 or 7:00 in the evening. Late in the evening the bidding does not go very high since many fewer people are there to participate. If and when I buy at the evening auctions, the prawns have to be taken home to be sorted, peeled, and cleaned. Then they have to be taken to one of the factories with which I have an arrangement to sell. Though there is much more money in bringing the prawns home, peeling them and then selling them, I cannot do it on a large scale. For that I must put up a peeling shed of my own and have a number of women working for me. Also, it is becoming very difficult to get someone to cart the prawns home at a reasonable price. I do plan to give up fish vending because it is both time consuming and low paying and concentrate on just buying of prawns and selling them away at profit without processing it.

For participation in the auction I need ready cash with me, though on resale the reimbursement is immediate. But when I sell directly to the factories as I do for the evening catch, I have to wait for three to four days on average to be reimbursed. The cash I generally carry with me runs between Rs. 300 and Rs. 500. During the monsoon months when the prawn catch is at its peak I can do with even more cash. In these months, there are times when I make a profit of Rs. 50 in a single day. But then there are lean months and also months when there is no business at all to do. All the same, I am now a full-fledged worker in my own right. In fact, I sometimes wonder if I should not cut down on my work so as to devote a little more time to my family, particularly to my two sons still in school.

Husband's work

For the last four years, our household has had four earning members including myself. Xavier has his own craft, a *kochuvallom,* and three different kinds of nets, including a few nets to catch lobster, which has a good market. The two gill nets he has are for sardines and mackerels. They are all made of nylon and cost somewhere between Rs. 2,000 and Rs. 2,500. Lobsters are something which have recently caught on as they have an export market. The lobster net is not very expensive except that it has to be replaced frequently. It lasts just six months. Moreover, you need a few of them so that they can be immersed in the sea at about one mile offshore where the sea bottom is rocky and lobsters are found. The lobster net is actually a sea bottom net whose meshes are of a rather large size. Xavier has three of them. The older boys, Titus and Joseph, go out fishing with not only Xavier, their father, but also on other crafts.

Xavier started working for the family that brought him up from a very early age. From what he has told me over the years, it appears that he used to carry water from the wells with water considered safe for drinking. It was only after pipes were laid under the Project to connect our three villages with Sasthancottah Lake that we stopped depending on these wells. I am sure he had to do a lot of other chores for the family. However, as he grew up, he was initiated into fishing. When I got married to Xavier, he was working as a coolie fisherman for other people's crafts, big or small. He was already considered a good fisherman. He was, therefore, not short of work, provided the weather was alright for fishing. Soon after Titus was born, Xavier negotiated for a second-hand *kochuvallom,* a small craft, from a neighbour in the village. He could raise the money from friends and relations because of his reputation as a good fisherman. Over the years, he has changed the boat several times, but stuck to the same small type. It is a more versatile craft and can be used for a larger number of days in a year. The craft he owns now was bought a couple of years back for a sum of Rs. 3,000. He borrowed some Rs. 2,000 by pledging our house and land and the balance was raised from friends and relatives to be repaid in small amounts from the earnings from fishing. He has not defaulted in the past, so his credit rating is good. Though he is completely illiterate, he is very methodical in his work. He takes great pains to maintain his crafts in good condition.

Managing the household

For the last few years, four of us from the household have been earning a living. The men, my husband and two sons, give me a major portion of whatever they earn. They do keep a portion to meet not only their daily personal expenses on tea and snacks, but also their contributions to chit funds. Each one of us subscribes to a separate chit fund. I subscribe to one separately. The management of the household budget is left entirely to me; with four earners, meeting our day-to-day requirements poses no problem. But new and major expenses have cropped up from time to time. The craft and nets have to be replaced often. The thatch of the house has to be redone once every two or three years. But the largest amount we needed to raise was for sending Titus to the Gulf. Thanks to my son, Antony, from my first marriage, we did not have much problem even then. Also, we all, individually and collectively, could contribute a little from our savings.

Looking ahead

The hard work that Xavier and I have put in all these 21 years has been reasonably well rewarded. We both are illiterate but all our children have been at school for seven to eight years. Given our backgrounds, both of us suffered from various difficulties but we have been able to give our children a better start. One thing I am sure of — without Eliyamma's open-hearted support we could not be where we are today. Our debt to her cannot easily be repaid. With both the girls now married and the boys on the threshold of better careers, I look forward to a brighter future. I would like to send my last two children, both sons, to college, if they do well in school, and build a brick house. I would like it to be provided with proper facilities like water, electricity and drainage. Several people here in our own village have been able to build good, comfortable houses. We too, I feel, ought to start building one, as soon as our debts are repaid. Xavier is not interested in having a mechanised boat, but when Titus is through with his job in the Gulf, he and Joseph would probably want to have one. However, that is a bridge we shall cross when we get to it.

PHILOMENA

The non-working wife

Name	PHILOMENA	No. of children lost under five years of age	Two
Village	Sakthikulangara		
Age	35	Family planning status	Sterilised after eight deliveries
Education	Nil		
Age at marriage	19	Occupation	Household duties
Dowry	Gold worth Rs. 300	Husband's occupation	Fisherman
No. of pregnancies	Eight	Ownership status	Owns a small traditional craft
No. of births in hospital	Seven	Type of house	Thatched hut on father's land
No. of births at home	One		

Introduction

I was born in a village called Puthenthuruthu, a small island village, a short distance away from Sakthikulangara where I live now. Even now, my village is not approachable by road. We have to use a boat or some kind of ferry to go back and forth from Sakthikulangara.

I come from a large family. Of the ten children, five girls and five boys, born to my parents, I was the third child. All of us were born in our house in Puthenthuruthu. My father was a fisherman owning a small craft, a *kochuvallom,* and a cast net. This is a small scoop net made of cotton used by the traditional fishermen of the area when the sea is rough and they cannot put their canoe at sea. This is a net that one can handle from the beach itself. My mother used to collect shells, clean and dry them and then sell them to be converted into lime. Even my mother's mother was a shell collector, though she also worked as a midwife attending to childbirths in our village.

Early childhood

I was never sent to school. There were no schools in our village and if one wanted to go, one would have to depend on the ferry. My parents were very hard up and did not see any need for educating children. So, none of us was sent to school. Some children from our village did go to school in Sakthikulangara by boat but they came from wealthier families. I stayed home and helped my mother with the housework and in

74

taking care of the younger children, of which there were plenty. Also, I helped my mother in cleaning and drying shells. Sometimes, I went out with her to collect them also. I attained puberty at the age of sixteen and at the age of nineteen, I was married off to Valerian, a cousin of mine living in Sakthikulangara. He was 23 years old then. We were married in the church at Sakthikulangara; the only dowry I got was a thin pair of golden ear-rings weighing 20 grams of gold worth Rs. 300.

Husband's household

In Valerian's house in Sakthikulangara, I was not with strangers. They were my relatives and used to visit my family before our marriage. That is how our marriage was arranged.

Everyone knew my father-in-law, as he took a very active part in the church. He was a strong and articulate man, proud of his awareness of politics and things in general. They were certainly being generous in letting me enter their family. They probably could have got a girl from a family doing better than us. Maybe, it helped that I was better looking.

My father-in-law is now 65 years of age. He had 12 children, but only 10 are living, as two of them (both boys) died, one in infancy and the other when he was 2–3 years old. The first one died when he was just two months, because of congestion in the lung. Of the surviving ones, eight are boys and two girls. My mother-in-law kept having children even after her sons were married and were raising their own families. My husband, Valerian, is their first living son.

Eight pregnancies

During the 15 years of my married life, I have had eight pregnancies, all resulting in live births. But I have only six children living. Both my first two children, girls, died as infants. I was expecting my first child two years after our marriage. I went to the government hospital, in Quilon City, for delivery. On the fortieth day, the child is usually taken to the church for baptism. But I lost my first child, a girl, on the thirtieth day itself. The Latin Catholic custom is that the couple should stay apart for a month. This is the minimum period of rest considered necessary for the wife and it is supposed to give her time to recuperate. During this time, she is given special herbal tonics, oil massage with hot baths and special food. I was also given all that. Within two months I was expecting again. This time also I went to the same hospital in Quilon, but had a premature delivery. The doctors felt the child was too weak. I went with my infant girl to my parents' home just to recover from both the mental and physical strain of all this. But the child caught whooping cough from one of my brothers. So I had to come back to my husband's place and take the child for treatment to the Benziger Hospital, a mission hospital, but in spite of all our efforts, the child did not survive. Around this time, Valerian and I decided to go and live in my village. Actually, my father had mentioned that he would give us some land as he had not given me any dowry. So we put up our hut on my father's land. But soon Valerian and my father had a big quarrel and just around this time when I was about to deliver my third child, he decided that we were not staying there any longer and that I should go with

75

him to his parents' house at once. But it was late in the evening, and we had to take a ferry. Half-way through, I started having severe pains. Nearby was living my grandmother who also was a midwife. She helped me deliver the baby, a boy. After fifteen days at my grandmother's house, I was moved to Valerian's house, because the child was running a temperature and had to be taken to the hospital for immediate treatment. It was found that the umbilical cord had become septic. The child took six months to recover completely, so he was baptised late. We call him Babu. He is now twelve years old.

When my fourth child was due, after a two year gap, I went to a private nursing home in Sakthikulangara. Earlier, for my first deliveries, I had gone to the government hospital. Both of the children born to me there did not survive. Then I had problems with the third one, delivered at home with the help of my grandmother. As my due date came closer I started worrying about where to have my delivery. I was irritable and would quarrel with Valerian and his people. Then one day he was so angry that he beat me up badly and I became really sick. I think he felt bad about it. So, it was decided that I should go to a private nursing home, though this would cost him a lot more money. My fourth child was a girl. She was baptised as Shirley. So far I had breastfed my children. But soon after Shirley's birth, I had problem with my breasts. So for a while I had to put her on diluted cow's milk. She was fed with a piece of cloth soaked in milk. But none in the family quite approved of it. So I switched Shirley back to breast milk as soon as the doctor felt that it was perfectly safe to do so.

I breastfed Shirley for a little over one year before I conceived again. This was my fifth conception. That depressed me a great deal. I had heard about family planning already and though as Catholics we were not supposed to use contraceptives or get sterilised, I felt that I could not go through pregnancies any more. But I had no courage to talk to anyone on this subject. When I went to the hospital for my delivery, my kidneys were found to be infected. This time, for my confinement I had gone to a church-run hospital. Keeping in mind my history of complications and my own state of health, the doctor there advised me to go in for sterilisation after delivery. I would have gone in for sterilisation if Valerian had been even half-willing. He was opposed to it stubbornly. After I delivered a boy, I returned home after three days. I was weak and had not quite overcome my problem with the kidneys; I got scabies and passed it on to the boy.

Valerian and I started having frequent arguments. I felt he and his people did not worry enough about my health. Also, I felt very weak. So I was packed off to my parents' home along with my three children. I was virtually separated from Valerian for almost three years. During this time my parents had to look after us. I was afraid that my children and I would become a permanent burden on my parents if I did not go back to Valerian.

Then Valerian came one day to take me home. Within less than a year of this I was expecting my sixth pregnancy. Not that I wanted any more children but I was now resigned to going through any number of pregnancies regardless of what happened to my health. I did not want to be packed off again. So after my sixth child within the next four years I had two more children. On the eve of my eighth delivery, I was very sick and felt really so low that I thought I would not survive it for very long.

The sterilisation

From my sixth delivery onwards, I had been going to the Project hospital in Puthenthura for treatment and confinement. There the doctors and other medical staff do not like women to have many children though they never send you away. Every time I went there in a pregnant condition, they would ask me if I would like my pregnancy to be terminated in view of my poor health. But who was I to say 'yes'? Valerian too would be asked whenever he was with me. He always said 'no'. I felt that he was really not convinced about the need. However, considering my condition during the course of my eighth pregnancy, he told the doctor that I could be sterilised if it was absolutely necessary for health reasons.

I stayed in the hospital for six days after my delivery and sterilisation. Soon thereafter, I was running a high temperature because the stitches had become septic. I had to be readmitted to the hospital for treatment. I never felt so weak as at this time. Now I have a nine month old baby with my health in utter ruin. I feel weak in the lungs and get tired very easily. But I must somehow keep home and cook for Valerian and our six surviving children.

Our hut

We live in this small thatched hut 15 feet by 12 feet, in back of the house in which Valerian's parents live. The land belongs to Valerian's grandmother. The hut was put up by us, some eight years back when Valerian brought me back from my home after a three year separation. The two-foot elevation helps to keep the rainwater from entering the hut. Of the two rooms, 8 feet by 6 feet each at the back of our 15-foot verandah, one is used as a store-cum-bedroom and the other as our kitchen. A part of the little space that lies in between the two rooms, 3 feet by 10 feet, serves as our prayer room. All Latin Catholic homes have their best room as a prayer room. You can see here our collection of calendar and poster pictures of Jesus Christ and Virgin Mary. I keep a small candle lamp burning there all the time. In the evening, all of us get together to offer our prayer to the Sacred Heart. In the store-cum-bedroom, Valerian hangs all his clothes on a string tied across the room, from one wall to the other. In fact, even my clothes and the children's clothes are hung there. This is the only way to air the clothes and keep them safe from rats. Hanging them on the lines helps keep the clothes out of everybody's way. Then the few extra fishing nets of Valerian are also kept in this room dumped in a corner. The one he is currently using is kept in a verandah corner.

My time

I spend most of my waking hours moving in and out of the kitchen. It takes some ten minutes to reach the public water tap for me or for my daughter Shirley to collect water. We depend on this tap for our drinking water. For washing clothes and cleaning vessels, I use the pond in front of our hut. Most of the area is only two yards above sea level, so it is easy to reach the water level. But the water is contaminated and has a high level of salinity. So, I use this water for all other purposes except for drinking and cooking.

I am the first to wake up in the morning except on days when Valerian goes out fishing in the early hours of the morning. I clean the front yard, bring some water and then go to the bushes for toilet purposes. We have three children going to school, Shirley, Solomon and Raju. Babu, my first son, has given up school already. Before she gets ready for school, Shirley helps a little in the kitchen. She is able to do more odds and ends after she gets back from school. I always keep some leftover rice and gruel from the previous night. Children have this for breakfast before going to school. Usually, Valerian goes to the street corner tea shop for his tea and breakfast. I make tea or black coffee just for myself and have it with the leftover rice. The children get ready by themselves and Shirley helps Raju who is just six years old. The school is not far away and is run by the church. The children can walk back and forth by themselves. Once they are out of my way, I attend to the two young ones. I am still feeding the youngest one on breast milk. It is not enough and I have to supplement it with some rice gruel.

I attend to washing of the vessels and the clothes after the children are taken care of. Washing clothes is a time consuming affair as the clothes are so dirty and I cannot spend much on soap. So you have to scrub and beat them hard. Washing clothes takes me two hours every day in the morning. Then I get back to the kitchen. I use firewood to do my cooking and kerosene for lighting the wicker lamps. Though there are no coconut trees on our land, there are some 20 trees on Valerian's father's land. These trees yield quite a quantity of dry shrubs that one can use for lighting a fire. The children collect them for me when they get back from school. But shrubs are not enough. We have to buy proper firewood as well. It is available from a corner firewood stall.

Husband's work and temperament

Things would not be so difficult for me if Valerian was doing well in work and was more cooperative and kind. He not only gets angry but usually his anger is turned on me. He feels bad that he is not doing as well as a fisherman as many others in this village. Over the years he has become even more bitter. While several others in the village, some very close relatives, own mechanised boats, Valerian has only a small craft, a *kochuvallom,* of his own. We have not been able to lay aside enough to improve our position. Last year his mood was even worse when the doctors diagnosed and declared him a diabetic. This upset him no end. How to avoid sugar and eat enough to do the kind of hard work that is necessary on a traditional craft, this was his problem. Then of course there was his addiction to liquor. He was strongly advised to cut down. But he is finding it hard to do that. On top of it all, two additional misfortunes occurred. In the heavy monsoons last year, our hut collapsed and we had to move into the house of Valerian's parents. We were really not welcome there, but there was no other alternative open to us. Then I fell sick and the doctors wanted me to be hospitalised and have my uterus removed. When I got back from the hospital, I was completely drained of energy and was at the mercy of my in-laws.

Not much love is lost between me and my in-laws. My mother-in-law has new daughters-in-law who have brought in much larger dowries and are healthier and possibly more helpful. My father-in-law just talks too much. He also spends a lot of money on drinks, possibly because he has wasted all the good opportunities that came his way. After all, he was one of the first to be allotted a mechanised boat when the Project started.

Own evaluation/prospects

With men like Valerian and my father-in-law, none of us women can have any voice. We must only reproduce children and take care of the home without protest. I would have liked to work and contribute to the family income in spite of my bad health, but they would not hear of it. I would have at least been less dependent. They feel that men at the boat yard are not only drunk and badly behaved, but also take advantage of women who go to work there. So I was never permitted to go to the boat yard.

Now that I cannot have children any more, I feel I can gradually overcome my health problems. Then, if Valerian is unable to take care of us completely, I shall be happy to go out to work. I am only 35 years old. So I am quite young. I see so many older women from our neighbourhood working and making money. I too would like to try. Of course, Valerian thinks that the children will soon start contributing their share. Babu, our eldest, has already stopped going to school. He can start going to the sea with his father. But I would like my other children to go to school for a longer time. How else can I make certain that I am taken care of well in my old age?

Summing up

I have six living children and more or less have been responsible for their care. Occasionally when I have been sick, either my parents or Valerian's parents have cared for them out of sheer necessity. The two main institutions about which I have some information are the school and hospital. I do not read the papers and we do not own a radio. Sometimes, I hear men talking to each other and that is the only source of information. Our main source of income is Valerian's fishing. We have no other source whatsoever.

MARY

Name	MARY	No. of children lost under five years of age	One
Village	Sakthikulangara		
Age	37	Family planning status	Sterilised after fifth pregnancy
Education	Nil		
		Occupation	Prawn peeler and agent
Age at marriage	20		
		Husband's occupation	Owns a small traditional craft and 10 different kinds of nets
Dowry	Rs. 300		
No. of pregnancies	Five		
No. of births in hospital	Two deliveries (including one which delivered twins)	Type of house	Owns a small brick house in a five *cent* plot
No. of births at home	Two		

I came to Sakthikulangara after I got married to Napolean in 1965. I was twenty years old then and Napolean was 24, just a few years older. Usually, the age difference between the boy and girl is greater than that between Napolean and myself.

I come from a fishing hamlet in Chavara village. Chavara is a predominantly Hindu village with coir, the coconut husk fibre, as the main base of economic activity. Even in fishing households, whether Hindu or Christian, while men were engaged largely in fishing, women, as was the case with my grandmother and mother, earned some money retting and defibring coconut husks. Both my sister, who is one and a half years older than me, and I learned to spin coir ropes. As young children, we would work for one of the many small rope producers in the village, spinning ropes of different strengths, at the *ratt*, the wooden spinning wheel specially designed for the use of coir fibre. Out of eight children, five boys and three girls, the two older girls were never sent to school. The remaining six went to school, though for varying periods.

My parents

Both my parents, Jerome and Augustina, belonged to the same village, Chavara. They were actually neighbours, but their marriage was an arranged one. My father was a ferry man transporting goods along the backwaters and my mother defibred coir and made coir ropes by herself. They had in all eight children. They are all alive. All the children were delivered in the hut itself with the help of a midwife and relatives.

I am the fourth child in the family. I have two brothers and one sister older than me. My first brother, Michael, still lives in Chavara with his five children and wife who also belongs to same village. Michael, who went to school for ten years, had a vasectomy, something that normally men among the fishing households don't do. He owns two Chinese nets and his wife works as a coir rope maker. Augustina, my older sister, is just two years younger then Michael. Though Michael went to school, Augustina and I, as I told you already, were never sent to school. Augustina is married and living in Sakthikulangara. They have been allotted five *cents* of land by the church under the rule that all families who were squatting for more than a certain number of years were to be given the right to settle. After her sixth child, Augustina was sterilised. Her husband is a fisherman and Augustina herself is engaged in buying and selling prawns.

My brother Yesudas, two years younger than Augustina, works as a boat crewman and his wife is a fish merchant. They have only three children but his wife has already been sterilised.

I am two years younger than Yesudas. Since I was never sent to school, I started defibring coir husks as quite a young kid. Whatever little I earned I gave to my mother. I also helped her in the house caring for my younger brothers and sisters while Augustina helped her with the household chores.

My other brothers and sisters

Of the three brothers younger than me, the brother immediately after me, George, has studied only for four years. He started going fishing in the backwaters, but later on switched over to a mechanised boat as a crew member. That is how he migrated to Sakthikulangara and stayed with us for a while. After he got married to a girl from Kadavoor, a fishing village near Quilon, they decided to live permanently in Sakthikulangara. His wife is very enterprising. She runs a shop selling not only tea but also groceries and fuel wood. Her parents are in this business in their village. They have three children. Now she has been sterilised. The two younger brothers also came away to Sakthikulangara first, and then tried to find jobs, in the Gulf, and eventually managed to go there. Antony worked for a while in Bangalore and then went to the Gulf. Later, he found a job for the younger brother, Lubis, also now in the Gulf. My younger sister Rita and her children stay with me while her husband is away on a job in the Gulf. My parents have also come away from Chavara. They stay with George, but eat their meals with me.

My marriage

My parents never really did well, though both of them worked. My father, though basically a ferry man, spent more of his time running an illicit liquor joint. One of his customers at this joint was an uncle of Napolean. It was through him that my marriage was fixed. It turned out that Napolean's parents had reservations about our family, mainly because of my father's liquor business, but they would not go back on the word given by Napolean's uncle to my father. Napolean's parents have been very generous ever since, considering the kind of reservations they had about my family and the smallness of the dowry given to me. I brought with me just 300 rupees in cash. After my marriage, I moved to Sakthikulangara to the house of Napolean's parents. I was not a stranger to Sakthikulangara. Already, my sister had been living there with her husband and children. In three or four years, we put up a small hut of our own on a plot of land belonging to Napolean's father.

Our hut

It is, as you can see for yourself, a very modest hut, all made out of thatch, walls as well as roof, covering an area of less than 300 square feet. The only room other than the kitchen serves as the household store.

I have lived here now for over ten years. I moved here sometime in 1970. Now, my father-in-law is obliged to sell this land to raise money for dowry to be given at the time of the marriage of his youngest daughter. However, this will not create any problem for us since we have already bought a five *cent* piece of land close to our present plot and are busy putting up a new house there. My brothers, who are working in the Gulf, have been helping us financially to put up our new house. We will soon have a comfortable brick house, with four or five rooms and also facilities like piped water, electricity and drainage. I am very much looking forward to our move to the new house.

Our children

Five children were born to us, two daughters and three sons. However, only four of our children are living now.

I was expecting my first child after two years of our marriage. Around the seventh month, I went back to my parents' house, and delivered my first child there. The very next day after delivery, I was bitten by a snake. I was given some Ayurvedic treatment immediately and I recovered. But it seemed to have affected the infant girl. My relatives felt that she also was poisoned as I was breastfeeding her. She died thirteen days after her birth. We did not have time even to take her for baptism. My oldest surviving child, a son, is now 14 years old and is studying in the eighth standard; we call him Prasad. We decided to follow the fashion and give our children Indian names rather than old-fashioned biblical names. He was born two years after my first delivery. This time I did not go back to my parents. Instead I stayed on in Sakthikulangara. A nurse working for the Project hospital looked after me when I was expecting. She also came to attend me during delivery. We were really desperate for money at that time so I was not given any of the special attention in terms of tonics (Ayurvedic) and baths that a woman is supposed to receive in the days immediately following delivery.

There was a gap of six years between our first and second son, who is now eight years old. He is studying in the third standard. I cannot quite explain the reason for the gap between my second and third delivery. I was not on any medicine, nor were we using any other spacing device. It just happened like that. This time I was under the complete care of the Project hospital. I went there quite regularly for my pre-natal check-up. I had my baby there and I went to the baby clinic thereafter for the immunisation programme. The baby clinic is also run by the Project hospital. We call this son Rajan.

My sterilisation

Before my fourth and last delivery, it was discovered by the doctors in the Project hospital that I was going to have twins. When the doctors asked if I would like to be sterilised after the delivery, Napolean and I gave our consent. That was in 1974. We both felt that four was quite a good number and that we did not want more children. Several women from the village had already undergone this operation, so there was nothing to be scared of. Even the church had started accepting sterilisation though publicly, it spoke and continues to speak against all forms of family planning. I must confess, however, that my health has not been well after the sterilisation operation. I get headaches and backaches quite frequently. Everyone here believes that these all are due to the operation. Still I am happy that I do not have to have more children. Instead, we can help those we have to grow up well.

Our household size

Our household size is somewhat unusual in the sense that it is much larger than our family. A number of my relatives have been staying with us from time to time. My younger brothers and sisters were anxious to come away from Chavara to find work opportunities here. As soon as prawn catches became larger, the whole area around Neendakara Harbour became the centre of work opportunities. How could I close my door on my own kith and kin when they came. I am sure that at the time of our need they too will help us. My sister-in-law, George's wife, is different. She is not sufficiently warm to them. So they all come to me. My younger sister, Rita, migrated here with her husband and their two children. She is still staying with us but her husband left recently for the Gulf. He has got a job there with the help of my brother, Antony, who has been working there for some years now. Antony had recently come home on leave and was staying with us for a few months. Then my youngest brother, Lubis, who worked in the Gulf for one year, had to come away when his firm there wound up. He is now trying for another job in the Gulf. Staying with me also is a 16-year old girl, Angela, from a neighbouring district; she helps me with my household chores. She has been with me from the age of ten.

It is true that we are quite crowded. Our present hut was never meant to accommodate 14 persons. During the daytime, however, there is not much of a problem. The menfolk usually leave home early in the morning and get back only late in the afternoon. Children go away to school. Rita, my younger sister, and I go away in the afternoon to the jetty to peel prawns. It is only in the night that you really feel the congestion but we have managed somehow. Next year, when we move to our new house, we shall feel the congestion very much less than now.

My first ten years after marriage

I must have started going out to work from the age of six or seven. As a young

83

child, I knew how to defibre retted coir husks, rotate the spinning wheel and later when I grew up I could spin two- and three-ply ropes. Until the time I got married, I worked for one or another *ratt* owner. Whatever I earned, I gave to my mother. After I got married and moved to Sakthikulangara, I did not go out to work for about ten years. I started having children straightaway, and also there was not much activity related to coir in Sakthikulangara. Defibring of coir had already been mechanised here and coir spinning was something that only a very few *ratt* owners in the village were involved in. Moveover, the wages in coir had remained so pitifully low that there was not much I could have contributed to the family kitty by working in the coir industry. Whatever coir defibring and spinning remained in Sakthikulangara was completely in the hands of Hindu women from the Ezhava caste. I don't recall any women from the Christian households in this village working for *ratt* owners. For the last five years, however, I have started going to work. It is easier now as even my two youngest children, the twins, are at school.

My domestic help

When I had twins, I really had a hard time. It was then that my brother-in-law brought the ten year old, Angela, a Christian girl from Alleppey, a town some 70 kilometres to the north. Her parents wanted to migrate to Goa in search of work and were short of funds. So we gave them 50 rupees and they left the child to work for us. She has been living and working with me for the last five years. She takes care of practically all my household work now. Thus I have a full-time housekeeper. We plan to get her married when we can find a proper match for her. That is our moral responsibility. Also, my sister Rita who, as you know, is living with us gives me a hand in all household chores. I do not really have to worry, therefore, about the running of the house, though the number to be taken care of is unusually large.

My present work

My elder sister Augustina, who too is married in this very village, has been engaged in the prawn business for the last ten years. So entry into the business was no problem for me. To be with Augustina was a great help, to start with at least. At the boat yard there is not only much physical jostling and pushing about, but also a lot of aggressive male talk that relatively younger women find it rather hard to take regardless of whom the talk may be aimed at. Most men at the jetty are, no doubt, from Sakthikulangara and known to us. Still it is different when you meet them at the jetty than when you see them socially. Probably when you participate in an auction, every one is on his own and has to stand his ground firmly. To gain acceptance as an equal bidder with men takes time, probably for all women. It is particularly so if you are young and on your own. Further, one has to deal with agents, peeling shed owners, auctioneers, peelers and coolies. All of them except peelers are men. We women have therefore to develop a thick skin in order to be successful in this type of work.

Initially, we women prefer to participate in small auctions. These consist of small lots. Strictly speaking, there is no rule against us participating in bigger bids. In actual practice, however, for large, expensive lots of prawns, where the bidding itself opens with Rs. 1,000, mostly men participate in auction. Women like me with modest cash on hand bid only in the smaller auctions, where prawns both smaller in quantity and of inferior variety are auctioned. But I cannot say that there is any segregation in work based on sex. While participation of women in the bigger bids may be close to 10 per cent, the ratio of men to women participating in smaller auctions is very much in favour of women.

It is usually around 1 o'clock in the afternoon that Rita and I go to the jetty. Each of us carries three to four hundred rupees in cash. This is the minimum working capital one needs to operate in a modest way. Many other women as well as men are there already. It gets very crowded by 3 p.m. when the boats come in quick succession to land their catch. The land including the jetty on the western side of the highway belongs to twelve Latin Christian families. All of these have become rich both because of the regular income from the use of their land by incoming boats and because of the enormous increase in the price of the land.

As and when necessary, Augustina, Rita and I pool our capital. Then it is Augustina who participates in the bidding on our behalf. Often, however, we operate separately to be able to bid in more than one auction since several auctions are going on simultaneously. When a bid materialises in my favour, I transfer it to the nearby peeling shed of the firm with which we have been having our dealings. Three teenage Hindu girls from a neighbouring village who have been working for us for some years now peel the prawns. The girls get paid according to the number of prawn basins peeled. On an average, they each make five rupees a day. While we don't pay for the use of the shed, we have to buy our own ice. However, we have to leave behind the shelled peels so that the shed owner can sell it as manure. We sell our peeled prawns to the export firms at a price, as I have already mentioned, according to the size and weight, but the prices keep fluctuating from day to day, indeed hour to hour, depending on the incoming catch. When the catch is good, the price is low. Each firm displays the price it is willing to pay for various sizes. On a good day, Rita and I can net as much as 75 rupees together after deducting our expenses for sorting, transporting, ice and peeling. This happens during the peak months of June to August when the catch is maximum. On a lean day, our earnings may be as low as ten rupees, even though on such days we try to do quite an amount of peeling ourselves. Then there are several days when there is little to buy, peel and sell. So one makes next to nothing.

The firm we deal with clears its bills only once every week and that is what creates headaches for us particularly during days of peak business. For, to be able to buy shrimps worth Rs. 1,000, in the course of one day, the weekly working capital we both require works out to be Rs. 5,000, a sum that is not always quite easy for us to mobilise. Both Rita and I subscribe to chit funds to keep our savings in a form that we can tap readily.

Napolean raises bank loan

The year 1980 has proved to be a year of distinct improvement for us. Napolean, my husband, was able to raise two bank loans, totalling Rs. 6,000, and buy a *kochuvallom* and a couple of nets. Now he owns, in all, ten different kinds of nets so that he can go out to sea more often than if he had only two or three nets. We have often thought of a mechanised boat, but it is still far too expensive for us. A new boat alone costs at least Rs. 135,000 and the gear would cost another Rs. 25,000. So it is clearly beyond our reach. Napolean could have enrolled as a crew member for a mechanised boat, but he is his own master now and prefers this status. After all, what he can make on a good day on his craft is not at all so bad. It is when one has no craft at all or an old boat which cannot be put to sea as and when necessary that one's position becomes difficult. Then you are no better than a landless labourer.

My daily routine

My first task in the morning is to see that the house is cleaned and the children get ready for school on time. We cook fresh rice for breakfast unless sufficient quantity is left over from the night's meal. The school is close by and the children come home to have their lunch. All the children who go to school, my four and Rita's one, have to be washed, bathed and dressed for school in clean clothes. Angela takes care of this, while Rita and I get breakfast going. After the children leave for school, Rita and I have our breakfast. We do not wait for the menfolk. But if any of them is there, he is served breakfast before we women sit down to ours. Men prefer to eat at the tea shops rather than share leftovers. After my breakfast I go out to do my daily shopping.

Lunch is the main meal we cook. The rice and tapioca we cook has to be sufficient to last the whole day including the night meal. We make a fresh fish curry again in the evening. Napolean leaves the house on most days at 5 o'clock in the morning and is back only around lunch time. He has his tea and breakfast at the tea shop, but lunch at home. Angela is there to serve him lunch if I am not there. Very often both Rita and I have gone away to the jetty by the time he is back. After lunch he likes to take a nap and the house is usually quiet for that. If he is at home for some reason, we take lunch only after he has been fed, a convention that all households follow.

Looking ahead

Both Napolean and I are virtually illiterate but we want to give a good education to the children.

With Napolean now owning his own craft and nets and my work going on reasonably well, it should not be a difficult target for us.

I think we have improved our status from where we started. We shall soon move into a proper brick house. If and when I need any additional funds for my business, or Napolean needs them for his work, we can be still reasonably certain of help from my brothers still in the Gulf.

I see much better days ahead for my children and also ourselves.

LILLY FRANCIS

The boat owner's wife

Name	LILLY FRANCIS	No. of children lost under five years of age	None
Village	Sakthikulangara		
Age	32	Family planning status	Had hysterectomy operation recently
Education	Two years of school		
Age at marriage	18	Occupation	Household duties only
Dowry	Rs. 6,000 and gold worth Rs. 1,400	Husband's occupation	Operates his own mechanised boat
No. of pregnancies	Six	Ownership status	Owns a trawling boat
No. of births in hospital	Six	Type of house	Brick house being built
No. of births at home	None		

Sakthikulangara is in my bones. Both my parents belong to this village; so did my grandparents and great-grandparents. Virtually every other family in the village is related to me. Almost all the marriages among Christians here take place within this village. This way not only can the family members keep in touch with each other but also the dowry money stays within the village. My husband Francis is from the same neighbourhood as our own. I had seen Francis before we got married but I had never spoken to him until after our marriage.

Marriage

I got married in 1967 when I was only 18 years old. We were married at the St. Britto's Church. Francis was 24 years old then. I had been sent to school for just two years. Since I was my mother's first daughter, it fell to me to take care of the housework and look after my brothers and sisters as soon as I was old enough to help. My parents gave away what was considered then a big dowry in my marriage. They gave Rs. 6,000 in cash and 70 grams of gold worth Rs. 1,400 in the form of jewellery. My marriage expenses amounted to over Rs. 10,000.

My brothers and sisters

My parents had eight children in all. Of these, three of us were girls and five boys. I have two older brothers but I am the first daughter. My mother never went to the hospital for her confinements and delivered all her children at home. All her eight children are living. Of these, five of us now are married, all three girls and two boys. I have three younger brothers who are yet to be married. My two older brothers are living separately with their families. Both of them are married to girls from Sakthikulangara. Each of them received a dowry of Rs. 5,000 in cash and gold worth Rs. 2,500. My first brother has seven children and the second one, four. They have not thought of limiting their families yet. Agnes, my younger sister, is married to a boat owner in this village. She has two children.

The cash dowry at my marriage was handed over to Francis's parents during the engagement ceremony that precedes the marriage by a few days. Gold was given to me in the form of jewellery. The unwritten rule is that the cash money is really for the groom to establish himself. Even gold brought by the girl is also at the disposal of her husband and his parents, as they can pledge or sell it during a crisis or use it as part of an investment to improve the family position. The understanding, however, in the case of gold is that the girl is entitled to get back the gold lent by her sooner or later, but there is no hard and fast rule about it.

Mother's dry fish business

My parents could give me a substantial dowry because they were doing reasonably well. My father owned a traditional craft and a couple of nets. However our prosperity rested on our mother. When I was young, my mother was a headload fish vendor going from one wayside market to another. Soon, she also got into the dry fish business. She would hire a coolie to cart the fish to the city market in Quilon where she had put up a permanent stall of her own. During the peak season, when fish is in a surplus quantity, she would buy it in bulk. All of us would help in drying the fish. This meant washing, cleaning and salting of fish before it was spread out in the sun for a day to dry. Small fishes like anchovies and silver bellies we could just sun dry without using salt. Mackerels and sardines we had to fillet and stack them in salt in alternate layers in heaps and wait for the water to drain out and then dry them in the sun. Bigger fish we would stack with alternate layers of salt in a trough and keep them for a day and then expose them to sunlight. Finally all these dried fish had to be packed in baskets with coconut palm leaf and made ready for transportation to the High Ranges and inland markets. This business venture turned out to be successful and very soon she was one of the wholesale dealers in dry fish, selling dry fish in bulk to merchants coming from the midlands and highlands where dry fish is a major item of consumption.

My mother had received some 15 *cents* of land in dowry at her marriage. It was on this piece of land that my parents built their hut where all their children were born and bred. Land fetched little price in those days; those with landed property would give a part of it in dowry if they couldn't give cash or jewellery.

My children

Once I got married, we set up a separate house. I have six children, and all are sons; the youngest is just a year old. I have had all my children in a mission hospital, known as Benziger's. It is not a free hospital, but it is considered the best hospital around. We prefer to go there because the treatment you get there is better than what you get at the government hospital. Though they don't fleece you, the mission hospital is expensive. It costs about Rs. 150 these days to have a delivery and stay for three days. In the 1970's, the hospital charge came to just about Rs. 50. Ever since then it has been consistently going up. Also, if I had gone to a government hospital, the doctors there would definitely have wanted me to get sterilised by now, since I have had six children already. However, government hospitals are absolutely free.

The general state of my health has not been so good. I have been on tonics for a few years now. My two and a half year old son is also rather weak for his age. We both are under treatment. I don't think I can go through another pregnancy, but I have been scared of the operation. There is no question of Francis undergoing an operation. This is unheard of in this village. Men in our community feel they would not be in a position to put in hard work once they go for this operation. Francis was not even keen that I should undergo sterilisation. In fact, he is not as concerned as I myself was about the fact that any more pregnancies could kill me. So I knew I would have to get over my own fear of the operation and to make up my own mind one day. I must confess that if I were feeling better I would not mind having a daughter also. You need at least one daughter in a family.

I had my first child in the very first year after our marriage. For a newly married couple to produce an offspring early is considered right and proper. If one does not get pregnant fast enough, one has to answer all sorts of questions. The family people start worrying. Childlessness is considered a great sin. Between the two situations where you do not have children and where you have too many, the latter is preferable. Remarriage among us Latin Christians is allowed only on the death of the spouse and not on the plea of childlessness.

My first son now is twelve years old. I have had more or less a child every one year and a half. All my six children have been breastfed. Four of them are going to school. The younger two are still at home under my own care. Recently we moved into my parents' house at the request of my father. Philomena, my youngest sister, was a great help to me once we moved in here, but now she is remarried and has gone to her husband's village. I am the only woman around in the house and I have my children as well as my father and brothers to take care of, as I have three brothers who are still to be married. Though there are six men around the house including my husband and father, I cannot ask them to clean, wash, cook or fetch water. It is never done. Nor would they be willing to help with household chores even if they were absolutely idle. The most men do is to take children out once they are cleaned, bathed and fed and do some shopping, and then only certain kinds of shopping. The strain of running the house is too much with my poor state of health. Anyway, we should be soon moving to our own house and then it might be easier to take care of just my family, though I do feel very concerned about my brothers and father.

Description of the house

We are living here on the 15 *cents* of land that were given to my mother as part of her dowry. It was on this piece of land that my parents built their hut and where all of us were born. We are rather cramped for space here, since I have moved in with my six children. We are now six adults and six children living in the house. When the land was given to my parents, there was just a thatched hut. My mother invested some money and put up a two-room brick house with a verandah and a kitchen. We have also a thatched enclosure to wash our utensils and to bathe. The house occupies only three out of 15 *cents* of land. There are about 25 coconut trees in the compound but nine of them have been destroyed due to neglect. Luckily we have an electric connection and all the rooms have doors and windows. We have a small pond from which we take water for washing and cleaning purposes. Since it is not protected water, we have to bring a couple of pots of drinking water from the water tap not far from the house.

Move to my parents' house

For the last two years or so we have been staying here in my parents' house with my family. I had to move in when two tragedies struck my family, one after the other, within a span of just one year. First, my younger sister, Philomena, became a widow within one month of her marriage. My parents had got her married to a young man from this very village who was already working a shrank, which means as a crew leader, on a mechanised boat. Philomena was given a handsome dowry of Rs. 10,000 in cash and 100 grams of gold in the form of jewellery. All told, it came to more than Rs. 20,000. Unfortunately, the marriage did not last for more than a month. During the months of June, July and August, prawns move in a big way into the coastal waters of Neendakara. But these are also the months most dangerous for fishing. The sea is most turbulent because of the south-west monsoon. So we have a number of accidents every year during this period resulting in loss of very valuable lives of young and daring fishermen. It is usually the more daring who venture beyond the safe limits and get trapped. Of course, let us face it, accidents and loss of life are a part of fishermen's lives. It is just too bad that it should happen to Philomena who was so recently married. Quite often these boats and the lives of fishermen are not properly insured so that the families of the dead do not get the right compensation. Even if the crafts are insured, they are not supposed to go during the monsoons. Loss of boats results in major financial losses. Men of course are seldom insured against their lives. In spite of that, boat owners are unscrupulous and encourage the crew to take great risks in order to make huge profits.

The shock of Philomena's widowhood was particularly felt by my mother who was already ailing. She had been a heart patient for some years. Within less than a year of this tragedy she passed away. A great deal of money was spent on her treatment, including hospitalisation. After my mother's death I had to move into my parents' house to stay with my father. Of course I had two sisters-in-law but it would not be the same. Two of my younger brothers were there and also my youngest invalid brother, who is still a heart patient, had to be cared for. Though I was not really well, they felt I still could be of help. Daughters are the ones people turn to during periods of emotional crises. With the addition of the eight of us, my parents' house has become rather congested and everyone is rather cramped for space. It is a brick house, but it has limited space with a total of not more than 150 square feet. Francis was not totally against moving here for several reasons; for one we would be closer to his parents' house as two of his brothers are working on his boat. Even my brother is working on his boat. Moreover, our hut was falling apart and we were short of funds as all that we had was invested in buying the craft. By moving in here, he felt he could keep a closer contact with the crew and commute to the boat jetty easily.

Philo's remarriage

Once we moved in, our first task was to see that Philomena was remarried as fast as possible. Among us Latin Catholics, not only is remarriage in such cases allowed, but also the girl is entitled to the return of the whole dowry. Where there is dispute, the church steps in and arbitrates. In fact the church records the amount of dowry given in each case. In Philomena's case, we got back all that had been given in dowry. The problem usually arises because to get a girl remarried, the dowry demanded is much bigger than in the first marriage. Philomena stayed at home for a full year and a half. Finally we found a suitable boy for her. He also works as a crew hand on a mechanised boat in a small neighbouring village. The dowry we gave has added up to Rs. 30,000. She comes to visit us often. Now we, Francis and I, are thinking of building a brick house for ourselves. We own a seven-*cent* piece of land on which we had a thatched hut. Because of disuse and lack of repairs, the hut now has fallen apart. We don't want to move as yet. With Philomena married and not close by there are no female members in the house. Two of my brothers who are married live separately with their families and are not anxious to move in. My second sister Agnes, who is married in this village, is also not in a position to help. So that leaves just me. Since Francis is not objecting to it seriously, even though we are cramped for space, I don't mind staying on here for some more time until we have built a brick house of our own.

Francis' work

Francis first started going out fishing at the age of 15. He studied up to the eighth standard. His father was a *vallom* owner and Francis went out to sea as one of his father's crew. Being the eldest son in a family of ten, probably he had to start work rather early. His other six brothers are better educated than him. When I got married to Francis in 1967, Francis had started as a deck-hand on a mechanised boat. However, he was never very comfortable on a mechanised boat as it invariably made him seasick. All the same he wanted to own one rather badly.

Francis, along with four of his brothers, became members of a co-operative society (Malsya Utpadaka Co-operative Society) and then applied to the government as a group of five for the allotment of a mechanised boat (32-foot trawler). The membership fee came to Rs. 155 for the five of them. Also, they had to deposit Rs. 14,000 as an advance along with the application. Francis was able to raise this amount with the help of his two brothers and one brother-in-law who are in the Gulf.

After a lot of running about, and greasing various palms, over a period of some 24 months, Francis and his brothers were allotted a boat. It cost Rs. 125,000 which has to be paid up in regular monthly instalments of at least Rs. 2,000. He has to pay seven per cent interest on the total cost of the boat. Thus he owns a mechanised boat now. Francis himself does not go out fishing. His brothers, along with my younger brother, Pius, constitute the boat crew. No one from outside the family has to be hired for the purpose. Francis takes care of all the transactions involved, including the maintenance and running expenses of the boat. He is trying to repay the loan as fast as possible so that the boat can then be transferred to our name at the earliest. That is the first priority for him. But at the same time he is laying aside some amount for the construction of our brick house. Luckily for us, Francis is not addicted to drinking and is not particularly keen on extravagant living in the manner of several of his compeers in this village. So he can save considerably more than others. In fact, if anything, it is my health and constitution which is a major drain on his finances.

Last month I had a major set-back and had to be rushed to the hospital. The doctors were firm and felt I would have to undergo a hysterectomy operation. We had no alternative left and had to give our consent. I stayed in the Benziger hospital for 15 days in all. The expenses came to some Rs. 3,000. So now the question of having more children does not arise. In a way I am glad it is all over. I feel weak but once I recuperate, I am looking forward to moving into our new brick home and taking better care of my family. With my health I cannot aspire to do anything more.

GORATTI

A deck-hand's wife

Name	GORATTI	No. of children lost	
Village	Sakthikulangara	under five years of age	None
Age	30	Family planning status	Has undergone sterilisation
Education	Three years of school	Occupation	Prawn peeling, taken up only recently
Age at marriage	17		
Dowry	Rs. 2,000	Husband's occupation	Deck-hand in a mechanised boat
No. of pregnancies	Three	Ownership status	Owns no craft
No. of births in hospital	Three	Type of house	Owns a new brick house on 13 *cents* of land
No. of births at home	None		

I lost my father when I was just two years old. He had gone out to sea fishing and was caught in a severe storm in which his craft capsized. He was with nine other fishermen on a large traditional craft, known by the name of *thanguvallom*. The plank-built canoe belonged to all the nine and was jointly owned. My father, who was 35 years old, and another younger relative of his, 22 years of age, both lost their lives. They found my father's body but they could not trace the young man at all. This is a hazard which all households of fishermen face. We have to accept it as a fact of life. In those days if a fisherman was lost at sea, that was the end of the story. In recent years, the state government has started paying compensation to the family. Also, there exist insurance policies which, however, only the better-off amongst fishermen can take out. When my father died in 1954, my mother had already four children and was expecting her fifth one.

Early background of my mother

Both my parents belonged to Sakthikulangara. My mother's father owned a *thanguvallom*. That was a mark of well-being among fishermen. My grandmother was not doing anything in particular besides housework. My mother, however, was sent to school for just three years. The church co-educational school was very close to their house but the parents never saw the need to send her for a longer period. It was not the normal pattern in the village for girls to be at school for a length of time. But even my father had been to school for five years only, enough for him to read and write reasonably well. When my parents got married in 1944, my mother was 20 years old and my father was 25 years old. She was given a dowry of Rs. 300 and jewellery worth

93

two rupees silver weight. They had been married for nine years only when the accident I have spoken about took place. Thus my mother became a widow at the young age of 30 years. On her rather young shoulders was thrown a rather big responsibility of bringing up thereafter four young children, including the one on its way.

Remarriage was ruled out

All of my mother's children were delivered at home. The first four of her children were all girls. One of these, her second daughter, died before my father's accident. The child, who was four years old, drowned herself when she was playing in the shallow backwaters. When her fifth child turned out to be a boy, and it happened so soon after my father's death, everyone including my mother herself felt that God had shown great mercy on her. They felt that now there would be someone to take care of her in her old age and give her both economic and social support. My grandparents, i.e., my mother's parents, and the parish priest suggested considering remarriage to my mother since she was still rather young. She felt, however, that she could not take such a step with four young children to take care of. The eldest child, Angela, was still only nine years old. Lilly was three and I was not even two years of age. Then she had an infant to take care of as well.

Meeting the crisis

Even after my father died, we continued to stay in the same hut, as the land belonged to us. My mother did not go out to work and her parents, particularly her father, and brother, lent her great moral support. About three years after her widowhood they learned that the locally-based government firm, Kerala Fisheries Corporation, was looking for women to work in its ice-cum-freezing plant. My mother was encouraged to put in her application. This was around 1957, i.e., four years after the Project had come into existence. There were not many applicants. Also, most women who applied were fishermen's widows, though my mother, I was told, was possibly the youngest.

My mother's regular factory job

For the last 25 years, my mother has been working in the government factory. In another few months, when she completes 58 years of age, she is due to retire. She now makes Rs. 400 every month and when she retires she will be entitled to a lump sum payment of Rs. 2,000. My mother is very sad that she has to retire in two months. She feels she is quite healthy and could go on working for some more years. She had taken the birth certificate from the church where she was baptised. The Hindu co-workers were able to understate their age for want of proper evidence. She feels she has to pay a price for being born a Latin Catholic. All the same, you cannot overlook the fact that it was because of the steady income she earned all these years that she could bring up her children without much difficulty. This regular job was a great boon for our family.

Our up-bringing

Angela, the oldest of the three surviving girls, gave up school when my father died. She had been to school for only three years. But even Lilly and I went to school for only three years when our turns came. The need to keep us in school longer was evidently not felt. We just stayed at home doing the house chores and taking care of our younger brother Gilbert while our mother was out at work in the factory. One thing my mother saw to was to keep the boy in school for the maximum period necessary. He, however, failed to complete his school-leaving certificate even after two attempts.

Our marriages and dowries

All three of us girls are married into families belonging to this village. When Angela was married off at the early age of 17, my mother was unable to give any cash in dowry. Instead, she promised to give her a part of the 12-*cent* piece of land which belonged to my father. The dowry transaction in these villages can take place in cash, land, gold or a combination of these. When she got married, the normal cash dowry stood around Rs. 3,000. The land my mother gave away was worth Rs. 5,000. Angela works as a commission agent and her husband works as a shrank on a mechanised boat. They have three children, one son and two daughters. She had all her children in the hospital, but so far has not gone in for any family planning measure. However, she has not conceived for some years now. So probably she does not see the need for family planning. But you cannot tell whether or not she will have any more children. After all, she has not yet crossed that point.

In the case of my second sister, Lilly, who also was married at the age of 17 years, my mother promised to give part of her land in dowry, the idea being that either the land or part of the sale proceeds should be given. Lilly's husband had a job in Bhilai, one of the steel towns in north-east India. He had to come away after an accident in which he lost a part of his hand. On his return to the village, he raised funds by borrowing from the banks and private parties and bought a new mechanised boat. He now manages the boat and Lilly runs a successful grocery store. They have five daughters. They gave up hope of a son and Lilly had a tubectomy after her last child. They are in the process of replacing their hut with a brick house.

I was the third girl and I too was married off early. It is my uncles, my mother's brothers, who found the match for me. Sebastian and I got married in 1969. It was at the time of my marriage that it was decided to sell off the 12-*cent* piece of land and recover the cash to be divided among the three sisters. I suppose you know already that dowry is very important for marriage in our society. Before the anti-dowry legislation, even the church was not against this practice. We even had the system whereby the whole amount was recorded with the church where a register was kept for this purpose. Earlier, a percentage of the dowry was payable to the church but that practice has been discontinued as many people would under-report the dowry transaction. This register is still maintained in the church so that in the event of any dispute one could always refer to it. In theory this dowry money is supposed to be for the bride; the practice here, however, is for the bridegroom to have the full use of it. Generally, he uses it for starting a venture of his own.

95

Sebastian, my husband

Sebastian was 21 years old when we got married. He had attended school only for two years. He had to start working at the age of 10 or 12 because his parents needed him to supplement their earnings. They had six children, four boys and two girls. Sebastian was the first son. Both his parents worked. Sebastian's father owned a *kochuvallom,* the small craft, and his mother worked as a headload fish vendor. The brother next to Sebastian turned out to be a very sickly kid. This was a great source of anxiety and expense. Ultimately, it was diagnosed that he had cancer and he died of it at the age of 24. All the other brothers and sisters of Sebastian could stay in school for a much longer period than Sebastian. One brother and one younger sister are also married now. At the time of his sister's marriage, a large dowry of Rs. 9,000 was given in cash and gold. Later, when Sebastian's brother's marriage was fixed, he brought a much larger dowry of Rs. 13,000 in cash and gold.

My husband's work

As I have told you, Sebastian started working at a very early age. When we got married, he was going out to sea with his father as well as with other fishermen. He was working hard to contribute as much as possible for the maintenance of his family. But his heart was in the mechanised boat. People who worked mechanised boats made more money, even though the period of peak activity was very short and concentrated. Luckily for him, quite a few of his relations had already acquired mechanised boats of their own. So Sebastian switched over as a deck-hand on a mechanised boat.

Constructing our own brick house

After I got married, I lived with Sebastian at his parents' residence for a period of six years. His parents stayed close to the old lighthouse where country crafts used to land their catch. This is also where the *valloms* are still berthed when not in use and men get together to dry out nets or repair them in the evenings. Though all *valloms* look alike, people have their ways of identifying them. With more and more people switching over to mechanised crafts which land their catch at the jetty, this old centre is looking more and more deserted.

The dowry money I brought with me was used by Sebastian to buy 13 *cents* of land not far from where his parents were living. We started saving money so that one day we could build a house on this land. Investment in a mechanised boat of our own appeared to be beyond our reach. So we thought in terms of a house of our own.

Working as a deck-hand, he made 40 to 50 rupees a day during the three months of peak activity. All deck-hands do that, but the general tendency is to spend it very largely in drinking and other wasteful ways so that in periods of lean activity they are generally reduced to a hand-to-mouth existence. Only a few more thoughtful ones who can think of the future for themselves try to plan some proper use of the income. Already, some households had changed their huts into brick houses.

In our village, the type of house you live in determines your status now. No longer does everybody stay in thatched huts. Many people have already built nice large brick houses. Once we had enough funds to start construction work we went to a local building contractor and got a plan drawn. The estimate was that the house alone would cost us Rs. 16,500. Sebastian mortgaged our land for Rs. 9,000. We calculated that we had access to Rs. 2,500 to start with and that the balance would be possible to raise from the chitties we were subscribing to. Actually, the total cost came to Rs. 17,500. Sebastian kept a detailed account of all the expenses. Over and above that, we spent Rs. 8,000 on electrical wiring, painting and furniture. Also, the house-warming ceremony involved a sizable amount; the only thing we could not afford was piped water and built-in toilets.

House-warming and pollu

On the completion of a house, it is the practice in our village to invite all friends and relatives for a house-warming party. At this party, each guest brings in a cash contribution towards the house according to his economic capacity. It is recorded in a proper way by the recipient family. These contributions together add up to a substantial sum so that the recipient family is able to repay the debts incurred by it during construction. Repayment of contributions received in *pollu* has got to be made in due course along with interest. In addition, one makes a small gift. There are no legally binding rules. The social sanction against default is so strong that default is simply unheard of. You keep repaying as the occasion arises. In case the giver has already built a house, then one can repay during a wedding in his or her family. There are enough occasions to settle these transactions. When we gave the house-warming party, we received some Rs. 30,000 in *pollu* contributions. Sebastian's brother sat down and noted down all the contributions in a register that we have kept very safely. I shall be very glad to show you the register. We could not only clear all the debts straightaway but also had some surplus. We bought a cow with the amount left with us.

Our new house

We moved into our new house sometime in 1978. It is, as you can see, made of kiln-fired bricks. We get these bricks from a kiln located about 3–4 kilometres from here, where bricks are baked in the traditional manner. I doubt if, barring a couple of very rich families in our village, anyone has built his house with wire-cut bricks. They are no doubt sturdier and better shaped but at the same time much more expensive. We used cement mortar. Cement was not in such short supply as at present. Now, the same house would have cost us a lot more because we would have had to buy cement in the black market. You can never get the allotment on time, however much you run around for it. We tried to economise on other costs as well. By going in for *jalli* walls, i.e., walls with holes spread out as in lattice work, we could dispense with windows. We opted for a red oxide cement flooring instead of mosaic flooring because the former is far less expensive. The item we did not economise on is the door at the entrance. We had to have a solid wooden door with a proper built-in lock. Also we got a neon light fixed in our living room, but the other rooms, including the kitchen, have only ordinary electric bulbs. I am quite fond of my kitchen. It has a platform for cooking and proper cupboards to store things. As you can see, I have almost all the local gadgets that one needs in a traditional Kerala kitchen for steaming, pounding and grinding activities. There are two things we still do not have in our house. One is a water connection and the other is a toilet. Sebastian and I discussed how we should build the house. In the course of its construction, I was probably around more often than Sebastian because he had to go away whenever the boat he worked for was out at sea. Of course, as is the case with everyone in the village, new constructions or major repairs are not taken up in the peak fishing season both because one has to be away at work and also because that is when it rains most.

The family

We live in the house just by ourselves, i.e., my husband and myself with our three children, two girls and one boy. My first child was a boy, Alphonso, who is ten years old now. He is studying in the fourth class. My second child was a girl, Anne. She is eight years old now. She is now studying in the third standard. The youngest one, also a girl, is four years old now and goes to a small nursery in the village where the children play and learn.

I was expecting my first child within one year of our marriage. I was just about 18 years old and staying with my in-laws. I came down with a severe attack of jaundice. This is a common problem here now. The general sanitation in our village has become worse over the years with the expansion in activities related to prawns. Prawn peeling sheds are spread all over the village with the result that you see mounds of peels rotting everywhere. Prawn peels decompose into manure, for which there is a good demand from farmers. As a result, however, there are many flies all through the year. Even if you keep the house absolutely clean, the chances of your getting exposed to infections are very high. I went away to my mother's house at her urging when I was five months pregnant. Since jaundice had made me rather weak, my mother wanted me to go to a private nursing home for delivery even if it meant expense. Already, there were several private nursing homes in Sakthikulangara, in addition to the two government-run hospitals within easy reach, one across the bridge and one in Quilon. I stayed in the nursing home for a week and then returned to the care of my mother. Ordinarily, she would have put me on Ayurvedic tonics, but since I had had jaundice we decided to stick to just allopathic medicines. We took the child for baptism only after he was three months old. Earlier, the practice was that the child was taken for baptism within the first ten days, but now this rule has been relaxed. We can take the child for baptism any time before it is six months old. I breastfed the child until I was expecting again after about 15 months. For my second delivery also I went to the same nursing home. Between my second and third children, the interval was four years. I delivered my third child also in the nursing home. Since I never felt well during the course of my pregnancies, I did not want to continue having children. With three children already, two daughters and one son, the time had come, I felt, to undergo sterilisation. Everyone in the village knows now that there are ways of limiting the family size. The radio and the movie houses carry this message. Moreover, the auxiliary midwife comes often on her rounds and was encouraging me to talk to Sebastian and have the operation performed. Sebastian was initially reluctant on the ground that the operation might disable me permanently, but he agreed when I told him that his fears were unjustified. It was not a new thing in my family, since my sister had undergone sterilisation after her fifth child. After our third child was six months old and when my periods started I went to the Quilon government hospital for my operation. I have had no complications after that and am at peace with myself.

Having a small family with all the three children in school, I have plenty of time. Housekeeping has been easy with a well constructed house. So I have started recently going with my sister to the boat yard to either operate as a commission agent or peel prawns for wages.

Brother's good fortune

Since my mother is going to retire soon, she may help me with taking care of the children. I do not think she will want to join us in business. She stays with my only brother, Gilbert, not far from my house. He started his career as a commission agent and is now an auctioneer. He and a friend of his raised a loan with a local bank and have bought a 36-foot trawler boat. He has also put up a modern brick house of his own. Now he owns his home and has a share in the mechanised boat. We are happy that Gilbert is doing well and is taking care of my mother well. Sebastian, my husband, is now working on Gilbert's boat.

Looking ahead

There is no doubt that we all had a good start because my mother had a steady job. Sebastian has been very hard working and as a deck-hand makes more than what is enough for our basic necessities. I am sure he would now like to buy his own boat. Maybe we can mortgage our land and raise the money. Once we get a mechanised boat and do better, we can think of sending our children to a better school. Not only are English medium schools much better, but also sending children there gives the family a higher status. Also, children not only learn to speak English better, but have a distinct advantage over other educated children in the village. These are our two major ambitions in life.

KADALAMMA

The boat manager

Name	KADALAMMA	Family planning status	Last child when 44 years of age, hysterectomy done after that
Village	Neendakara		
Age	60		
Education	Nil	Occupation	Dealer in marine products and auctioneer
Age at marriage	19		
Dowry	Nil	Husband's occupation	To start with, a fisherman, now a trader in fish
No. of pregnancies	13		
No. of births in hospital	Five	Ownership status	Owns two mechanised boats–one gill netter and one trawler
No. of births at home	Eight		
No. of children lost under five years of age	None	Type of house	Owns a brick house on 40 *cents* of land given for fishermen by the government, has defaulted on monthly dues.

Everyone at the boat yard in Sakthikulangara calls me Kadalamma. This is the way we refer to the sea. It means the sea mother goddess. After all, it is the sea that nourishes and sustains us. She is like a mother to all of us fisherfolk. We are totally dependent on her bounties for our livelihood. I am called by this name more out of fun. Very often when I am waiting at the boat yard for my husband and sons, I pray loudly imploring the goddess to see that they come back safely with a good catch. It is within everyone's hearing. I probably articulate the inner feelings of everyone. The difference is that they pray silently. The sea mother goddess has always obliged me and I don't mind if people have a little fun at my cost.

You must understand that all of us in these villages have a nickname. It is usually coined on the basis of the most obvious negative aspect of our personality. Also, we need these nicknames because the same formal names occur so frequently that some additional identification does help. Among us Latin Catholics, the practice has been to have names that are of Portuguese origin. And our stock of such names is very limited. Names like Napolean, Sebastian and Jacob occur several times over. The younger generation has now moved to more Indian names, taken from Hindi movies. All my grandchildren have such names. It took me a little time to adjust to them but I must confess that these are simpler to pronounce and sweet sounding.

Growing up

My parents had in all ten children of whom only six survived, five boys and one girl. I cannot quite tell you how their four children died. All that I can say is that I do not remember any of my brothers and sisters who were grown up and then lost. None of us went to school. My parents were illiterate and so were we.

I grew up taking care of the housekeeping chores and raising my young brothers from a very young age. There was plenty of work to be done, the hut had to be swept, water brought from the well, vessels washed and cooking done. Then the menfolk had to be fed in turns as all of them would not arrive at the same time. When I was around eight years old, I started defibring coir husks. Sakthikulangara had a sizable coir defibring activity at that time. Now they have a mechanised defibring unit employing just four to five women. Moreover, the Latin Christians have moved away from this occupation. A few Hindu families only are now involved in this activity. During part of the year, I used to collect shells with a scoop net. These shells would then be sold to a merchant who would have them crushed into lime powder.

My marriage outside our village

I was born in Sakthikulangara, but got married in a family from the neighbouring village of Neendakara. Since both the villages are physically so close and consist largely of Latin Catholic fishing households, there has been a limited amount of inter-marriage. Of course, people from Sakthikulangara always had a little feeling of superiority. Fishing households in Sakthikulangara owned land and had business interests and education. Once the Project came up, they moved ahead even faster and the village became prosperous. Because of their relative prosperity, they always preferred the children to marry within their own village. This was one way of keeping the money within the village and checking that the money was not being misused. In recent years, therefore, this tendency for Sakthikulangara parents to marry their daughters within the village has become even more pronounced.

I did not belong to an affluent fishing household. My father was only a coolie fisherman and my mother a headload fish vendor. Added to it, as a girl, I was free with young men of the village, so I was looked down upon. My parents could not find the right match for me in Sakthikulangara. I was considered immoral as I knew most of the young boys in the village. Ordinarily, grown-up girls do not talk to boys until they are married. My parents came to know of a young man in Neendakara who came from a very poor family. John was never sent to school. Evidently, even feeding him at home was a problem for his parents. He was brought up by the parish priest. His job was to carry the tiffin box of the parish priest wherever he went in the course of travels within his parish. There would always be something left over after the priest had finished his lunch. That was for John. Then, of course, he lost the job.

At the age of 12, he started going to sea for fishing. He started with the hook and line and soon started using various types of nets. Then he joined his father and brothers in fishing operations. When I married John, he was considered a good fisherman, though still very poor.

Our thirteen children

Within a year of my marriage in 1941, I was expecting my first child. I went back to my mother for my confinement. The child was delivered in the hut and its arrival was announced with the beating of the floor with fronds of the coconut palm. Three beatings meant the arrival of a male child and one for the arrival of a female child. I was completely under traditional care, in terms of tonics, massage and bath. The fifth day the child was taken to the church for baptism.

Among the Latin Catholics, no special period of separation is laid down to keep the couple apart. I have now been married for 40 years, and have produced 13 children. All of them are living. The first eight of my children were delivered at home and the subsequent five at the Project hospital. Every time I went to the hospital there would be pressure from the nurses and doctors there to persuade me to put an end to my further pregnancies. I was firm and refused to use any kind of protection against pregnancy. I had no problem having children. I was healthy and was prepared to have as many as God had willed for me. We have a large family of eight sons and five daughters. I had my last child when I was 44 years old. After that I had my uterus removed when the doctors told me that I was going to have complications. I went for my operation to the Benziger Hospital in Quilon town. I breastfed all my children and never had to buy any tinned milk. I nursed all of them. If there was any problem with my milk, I would buy cow's milk and dilute it with water. When the infant was too small, I would soak a piece of cloth and squeeze the milk onto the lips for it to suck. I never used any feeding bottle.

My working life

All these 40 years I have been married, I have been working for a living. To start with, it was a sheer necessity that I should make my contribution to the family's subsistence expenses. Later, however, as things started improving there was not such great pressure, but I felt restless just sitting at home. To begin with, I sold fish caught in Neendakara itself. Later, I started going to Sakthikulangara. There I had many contacts of my own. Many young men whom I knew as a girl would oblige me and sell me fish at reasonable prices. Other fish vendor women soon became jealous and stories started circulating that my old boy friends were trying to entice me for sexual favours. Naturally, it made John angry. So I decided to give up fish vending altogether.

Instead, I took to collecting shells. This is an occupation normally pursued by young girls. I must confess that soon I got to know the shell merchant rather well. I not only collected shells myself but also got several young girls to work for me. In this way, I could deal in large quantities and make a good income. Again, rumours started spreading and when they reached the shell merchant's wife there was a commotion. The parish priest had to intervene. That meant the end of my shell collection.

I tried to go back to fish vending, but it was hard. I did not wish to use my old contacts. No doubt all the men I knew as a girl were now married, but they would, I am sure, still have helped me. However, having burned my fingers already, I decided not to go to any of those men for any fish. For quite some years, it was a real struggle making just a couple of rupees after a whole day's hard work vending fish.

Our first break and boat

It was around this time in 1957 when we were really struggling that our first break came. The Norwegians had been around for some time already. After an initial period of experimentation, it was announced by the government that boats would be distributed through the Co-operative Societies. Many fishermen sent in their applications and so did John. One fine day, a card arrived from the Co-operative inviting him for an interview. Receipt of the card, I recall, was itself a matter of great excitement among us. John appeared for the interview and was told by the President of the Co-operative that for a nominal payment of Rs. 5.25 a boat would be handed over to him. John promptly cleared the formalities, which were rather straightforward, and became an owner of a small mechanised boat.

This was a 25-foot boat with just an 8 horsepower diesel engine. He was given training to operate the boat at the Project boat building yard. John's was one of the 67 boats distributed at that time. The understanding was that 50 per cent of the cost price was to be paid back in easy instalments. Of course, neither John nor others really tried to pay back. Every one took it as just a routine request which the government would never quite enforce. John made good use of the boat. He worked very hard, determined as he was to make success of the break we had thus got.

Things started really brightening for us only when we purchased our second boat in 1962. This was a second-hand 30-foot boat, with a 16 horsepower diesel engine and it was capable of operating a small shrimp trawl net. This brought in very good catches. There were some days when John made Rs. 70 to 80 per day in-season, after meeting all his expenses. It was around this time that the word went round that the 'chakara' season was on in the area around Alleppey to our north and people were hauling the naran variety of prawns. John went off immediately and stayed there for two weeks. He came back loaded with money and gifts for the family. I was angry that he had not bought any gold. Our first daughter was grown up and ready to be married off. Shouldn't he have thought of it and brought some gold which we would have to give in her dowry? Immediately, he decided to go back to fish for some more days. This was when we felt the most prosperous in our life. Not only were we able to marry off our daughter but also we bought ten cents of land in the village. We gave her a dowry of Rs. 2,000 and 40 grams of gold worth Rs. 540.

I gave up headload fish vending and started going to the boat yard to wait for our boat to return from the sea. As soon as the catch was landed, it had to be auctioned and money recovered, and shared. Though our sons also joined the crew along with John, sharing had to be done if even one of the crew was not from the family. Since the boat was in the name of John, he got not only his share as crew-hand, but also as the boat owner. A boat owner gets sixty per cent and the rest is shared by the crew. I participated fully in the supervision of all transactions involved after the fish was landed by our boat, so John and our sons did not have to worry about them.

Within a few years of his acquiring the second mechanised boat, our first Project boat had an accident at sea. John was far too adventurous and went to distances few others would dare go, particularly when the weather was rough. We almost gave up hope for him and our sons. Luckily, they were all picked up by the rescue team that went out in search of them. But the boat was a complete wreck. We sold it off and replaced it with another similar new boat with the help of a bank loan. John gave up fishing thereafter and switched to trading in fish. Soon he became very good in the buying and selling of fish and was able to make a reasonable profit. Ever since, I have been handling the affairs of the boats. With John completely off work for a few years now, the responsibility of overseeing the business of the family is completely on my shoulders.

A working day in my life

I wake up early, much before sunrise. After a wash, my first job is to go to the boat jetty in Sakthikulangara. It takes me 15 minutes to get there. But on my way there, I stop for tea. Being 60 years old now, I do not have to worry about where to have tea. Women younger than me have to be more careful and avoid tea shops popular with men. The gill netters go to sea only in the morning before sunrise and return to shore in the afternoon. I am always there before our gill net boat returns to supervise the auction proceeds of the fish at the jetty. By ten o'clock most of the work is over and I go for my breakfast to one of the few tea shops close to the jetty. Then I go back home. The running of the house is now in the charge of my youngest daughter-in-law. Between my daughter and daughter-in-law they have divided the chores. We take our lunch around noon. The menfolk eat first and then it is the women's turn. Again I go to the boat yard in the afternoon also. Our second boat, the trawl netter, comes back from the sea then. Around seven in the evening, all the family members gather to offer prayers and then eat dinner. Again, men are served first, then the women. I do not take any part in the household chores. My hands are full looking after the business operations of our two boats. In addition, I participate in buying and selling prawns. I find work at the jetty quite exhausting, particularly now that I suffer from high blood pressure. I have to spend quite some money on medicines every month. Haven't they become expensive? When a doctor knows that his patient can afford to buy expensive medicines, he probably prescribes for you only such medicines.

Operating costs

Every trip of the mechanised boat costs about Rs. 500. If the boat has to be operated for about 12 hours, we need diesel fuel worth Rs. 150. During the peak season, which lasts three months every year, I get between Rs. 750 and Rs. 1,000 per day. During off-season, our income after covering costs is reduced to Rs. 300 on the days the boat is taken to the sea, which itself is not often.

As I told you, I do not just auction what we get as our own catch; I participate also in the buying and selling of prawns and fish.

Originally we had put up one thatched hut on a 5-*cent* piece of waste land belonging to the church. John had been supplying fish free to the clerical staff for some years, so they obliged him by not objecting to our squatting on church waste land. In order to put up the hut we had to fill up this land with lots of earth to raise its level. For quite some years we stayed in this hut. Only in 1963 after John made some quick money did we think of buying our own piece of land. I calculated that to provide each son a 5-*cent* plot to build his house, we needed 40 *cents* of land. So whenever there was a little extra cash on hand that was not needed for our business operations, we would add on to our land. As a result, we own 40 *cents* of land. Our present house was completed in 1964. It has, as you can see, walls made of burnt bricks laid in lime mortar. The roof is wooden, however, being built with coconut and anjili, the local equivalent of a wood similar to white cedar. All our doors and windows are made of the same wood.

Our house occupies an area of 23 feet by 16 feet. The rooms are 13 feet high. To the front and back we have a two and a half foot verandah. On the south side, which is our back side, we keep all the nets. On the north side we sit down for relaxing and sleep during the dry days. I needed all the space with thirteen children. Now of course eight of my children are married and only five are left. Of these, four are boys and one is a girl, whose dowry we must provide.

About our children

My oldest child, a boy, is 37 years of age and the youngest, again a boy, is only 13 years old. We sent all our children to school, but none stayed in school long enough to complete the full course. None was really interested in studying, neither boys nor girls. The longest any one of them has stayed in school is Sebastian, our twelfth child. He studied up to the ninth standard. I know that some people in the village look down on us, thinking that with all our prosperity we have not educated our children. Other families which have done well have sent their children to colleges while our children have not completed even their school education. Looking back, I wish we had pushed our children much harder to go through school, but we had little time for it. Neither of us had any time to relax. Moreover, I was having a new child practically every 18 months.

Silva, the first son

When Silva, our first son, got married to a girl from Sakthikulangara, he got Rs. 1,000 as dowry and some 24 grams of gold, which were worth Rs. 400. They have four children now, two boys and two girls. The first two were delivered at home. For the third one, my daughter-in-law went to the mission hospital in Quilon. When she conceived again, they decided to call it a day. So we had to take her to the Project hospital for delivery and sterilisation. The decision to get sterilised was altogether that of my son and his wife. I did not feel like getting in their way. All their children are going to school now. They live in the same compound with us but in a separate house. Silva is the driver of our trawler boat. Though the boat is in Silva's name, as is the bank loan, I manage the boat's affairs and handle all the boat's finances. Silva gets his share of the boat's earnings in his capacity as driver. Silva's wife goes to the jetty and deals in the buying and selling of prawns. She works independently of me and retains whatever money she makes.

Ambrose, the second

Ambrose, the second son, got a slightly higher dowry of Rs. 1,500 and 32 grams

105

of gold. His wife had five children, one of whom died within just the last seven days. Now she is expecting again. They too live in a separate hut in the same yard. Ambrose has become a problem son, having become an alcoholic so early in his life. I have to support them financially, but it is worrisome that they cannot manage on their own. How long will his brothers support Ambrose once we are not around? This question has got to be faced by him before it is too late. His wife is not working as her children are still rather young. I have not advised them to consider sterilisation, but looking at Ambrose it would be in their own interest if they do not have any more children. I would then like to take his wife to the boat yard and initiate her into the business of buying and selling prawns. There is considerable possibility for women to make a decent living in this type of work.

Our third and fourth sons

Lazar, our third son, decided to marry on his own. He met the girl when he went with our boat to Alleppey. So there was no exchange of dowry. If I had fixed up his marriage, we would have received a good dowry for him. But he did not listen to me. Though he is not educated as he never went to school, he makes a good crew-hand on a mechanised boat. They have three children, two boys and a girl, all delivered in the hospital. She has been sterilised, but is not doing any work. She stays with us and looks after the house, but they also have a separate hut in this yard.

Next to Lazar comes Michael, who is the most competent of all our boys in handling mechanised boats. He wanted to marry a girl he liked when he was just 18 years old. I refused to hear anything of that sort. Later, I bargained with the girl's parents and when they agreed to give a dowry of Rs. 11,000 and 40 grams of gold, I gave my consent. Just when the negotiations were about to be completed, we found out that the girl was already four months pregnant, not from Michael. That would have led to a lot of talk among people in the village, so we withdrew our consent. Immediately, we got Michael married to another girl for the same amount of dowry. They have two children now, one boy and one girl. His wife is not working. They too stay in a separate hut close to us on our land.

After Michael come my daughters, Rose and Tracy. Rose did not go to school for more than four or five years. Instead, she would go out with girls of her age in the neighbourhood collecting shells. Also, she helped me in taking care of the house. When she was 17, we got her married to a boy, called Lawrence, from a neighbouring village, Perinad. We gave her Rs. 2,000 in cash as dowry. She delivered four children but her last child died just two days after it was born.

My next daughter, Tracy, is 28 years old. Although even she did not show much interest in school, I did not allow her to go out collecting shells as soon as we started doing a little better. I got her married at the age of 18 to a boy of 25 years from Sakthikulangara. We gave away Rs. 6,000 in cash and 56 grams of gold as dowry. She has three daughters now. She wants to have a son before she stops having children. Her husband, though a good boat-hand, is very fond of drinking and gambling. Also, he goes to movies practically every day. So there are far too many quarrels between my daughter and her husband. He is short of money all the time and when she asks him for money to run the house, she gets beaten up. I do help her a little, but not much. He expects a lot more, seeing that we are doing so well in our work.

106

The two sons, Albert and Henry, who came after Tracy, work also as boat-hands on our own boats. Both of them are now married and living separately, each in a hut of his own. Albert has two children, and Henry has one child. Their wives are not going out to work.

Jacintha, our third daughter, is 28 years old. We got her married rather early, at the age of 16 years. Her husband is a fish merchant. We gave her a dowry of Rs. 12,000 in cash and 70 grams of gold. She has had three children, all sons, already. One son, aged one year, was drowned in the bathwater. She plans to stop pregnancies after her fourth child. Although Jacintha's husband is doing reasonably well, he squanders a lot on drinking. As incomes have increased in our village, people have taken more to drinking. Already Jacintha's husband has acquired the reputation that he never repays the money he borrows.

Christina and Lourdes, are our fourth and fifth daughters, are also married. Christina was married in 1980. I had to give Rs. 10,000 in cash, Rs. 1,000 as pocket money and 72 grams of gold in dowry. I do not believe in keeping girls unmarried for long. Then there is the risk of their choosing men themselves and foolishly. In the case of my daughters, I did the selection of boys for them. True, even selections made by parents can go wrong. Tracy's case is a clear example. But I have no doubt that the girls can go wrong more than their parents in the selection of their husbands. I hold the same opinion about the selection of brides for the boys. It should, in my opinion, be left to the parents.

Lourdes has finished the sixth standard and is not going to school anymore. I have to get her married, but right now she is looking after the house. I have to save for her dowry.

My youngest son George is only 13. I would like him to study in school a little longer. Let us see if it works that way.

Looking ahead

No doubt we have come a long way, but it was by dint of hard work put in by both my husband and myself that we have been able to achieve our present level of well-being. It is reflected in our present assets and income. After we both are gone, the assets will belong to our eight sons. The daughters have already been given their share in the form of dowry, so they have no legal claim on anything more. But we cannot altogether wash our hands of our daughters, particularly when they are in difficulties. Take the case of Tracy. We shall have to leave something for Tracy so that she can bring up her family in spite of her husband's wasteful habits. Brothers are supposed to protect the interests of their married sisters but knowing my sons as I do, I cannot leave my daughters quite to their brothers' mercy. As for our own old age, I am not worried. I still have full control over our business and hope to exercise it until we die.

BEATRICE

The prawn dealer

Name	BEATRICE	No. of children lost age under five years of age	None
Village	Neendakara		
Age	41	Family planning status	Underwent hysterectomy after third child
Education	Nil		
Age at marriage	21	Occupation	Trading in prawns
Dowry		Husband's occupation	Formerly an employee of a prawn company, now helps in family's prawn business
No. of pregnancies	Three		
No. of births in hospital	Two	Ownership status	Owns two mechanised boats
No. of births at home	One	Type of house	Wooden hut on five *cents* of land

After you pass the highway bridge on the Ashtamudi Lake, you have to walk about a hundred yards past the huge stone wall, enclosing the area on the west side of the highway, earmarked for the proposed Neendakara port. You come thereafter to a few grocery and tea shops near the road bend and then a roadside water tap. At this point where the highway turns right, a wide dirt road takes you to the left. This dirt road was built by Thangal Kunju Musaliar, a rich cashew merchant who used to frequent this seaside beach to spend the evening.

Within a distance of 20 yards, the dirt road takes a sharp left turn leading on to the beach. Here, on the right side of this bend stands a thatched hut which, unless one is careful, can easily be missed. Both the roof and the walls are made out of coconut palm leaves. The back of our hut is towards the road and our verandah faces a small lagoon, on the other side of which is the highway. Most of the lagoon is so well covered, from one end to the other with water hyacinth called 'African Payal', that one can hardly see the water. It gives one the feeling of a green walkable stretch.

Our hut

Our whole hut stands on a raised platform, about two feet above the ground so that even during heavy rains water does not enter the hut. The platform is made out of mud and rubble. They are beaten hard to provide a solid base. Then the surface is plastered with a mixture of clay and burnt coconut husk. It is this which lends it a duel dark colour.

The largest room of our house, 9 feet by 8 feet, is the family's bedroom. The verandah in front of the bedroom, 8 feet by 3 feet, serves as our sitting room. The only item of furniture in our verandah is a long, narrow wooden bench for visitors to sit on. Of a number of pictures you see on the inner wall of the verandah, quite a few are of Christian saints. But there are also a large number of family photographs we have collected over the years. They are taken usually on the occasion of weddings and funerals of relations and friends.

You enter our bedroom from the verandah through a proper wooden door. The small chimney lamp nailed near this door burns on kerosene oil. The door has a proper latch and I can lock it both from inside and outside. Inside our bedroom, we have built in the left-hand corner a small altar with a colourful picture of Jesus Christ. Next to the altar is a single-door wooden wardrobe. The wardrobe is divided into two portions. The top half has three shelves to keep one's clothes. In the top shelf are kept my six cotton sarees and blouses, all neatly folded along with my wedding saree which lies at the bottom. In the lower half of the wardrobe are three drawers where our children keep their books. Next to the wardrobe is a table which Jacintha, my eldest daughter who is studying in college, uses for studying at home. The altar, the wardrobe and the table take up, as you can see, the whole of the left side of the bedroom. The large bed close to the back wall has wooden legs and a wooden frame. The inside of the frame is done in cane. Such a bed could cost quite a lot now, but we bought it long ago. In the night, we spread out mats on the floor for our four children to sleep. We, the parents, sleep in the bed. Francis, my husband, hangs his clothes on the clothes-line running from one end of the right wall to the other.

Our kitchen

You can enter our kitchen from the bedroom, but you can enter the kitchen from outside as well. It is around 5 feet by 6 feet in area. I have three mud stoves, five or six mud pots and a few aluminium and steel vessels, plates and ladles. Steel vessels are expensive and we take great pride in possessing them. In the two shelves which we improvised by tying up two wooden planks to the poles which support the wall, I keep all my spices and groceries in cans of various sizes. Our kitchen has a small verandah of its own, facing the lagoon. Here we stack our firewood along with the large aluminium pan and basin that I take to the jetty when I go there for buying prawns.

The public water tap is just a five minute walk from our hut. Usually, the children fetch water for me, for bathing as well as for use in the kitchen.

We have no latrine of our own. Since there are very few houses in the village with latrines of their own, there is nothing unusual about our doing without one. In fact, everyone, men and women, adults and children, go out to answer the call of nature. All go to the sea-front. The waves are supposed to wash away the dirt. Areas are marked separately for men and women. So there is little potential for invasion of privacy between the sexes.

Very close to our hut are other huts. Our immediate neighbour is a very old Hindu widow living by herself in a small one-room thatched hut. She makes her living by defibring retted husks and making coir ropes. She is mentally disturbed and at times keeps talking to herself for hours on end. In the other hut next to ours, an old couple lives with a mentally deranged daughter of 35. They are Latin Christians and related to me on my mother's side.

My husband changes his occupation

Francis, my husband, is now 48 years old. He is known in Neendakara as Mukadu Francis, because he comes from Mukadu, a nearby fishing village, half way between Neendakara and Quilon. While Francis's grandfather was dealing in coir and copra (dried coconut kernels), Francis's father was a ferry man.

I was just 21 years old when we got married. We were married in the St. Sebastian's Church in Neendakara which, as anyone will tell you, is one of the oldest churches in Kerala. Francis was 28 years old and working as a tailor in his own village. I moved to his parents' house there, and stayed there for three years before we decided to move to Neendakara. That was in 1963; by then the Norwegian Project had been there already for ten years. There was a lot more activity in Neendakara than anywhere else in the neighbouring villages. Several of my own relatives, four of my five sisters, were living in Neendakara and their families were doing well in whatever work — all connected with fishing — they were engaged in. Francis had been a tailor since the age of 15 and knew little fishing. Still he had not been doing well as a village tailor. He thought, or was persuaded to think, that he might make a better living in Neendakara. Moreover, I was not getting along well with his people. So my father put in a word for Francis with a cousin of his who already was well established as a seafood processor and exporter. As soon as Francis got the job, we moved to Neendakara. Francis sold off his sewing machine after a couple of years. That was the end of his tailoring. He and I hoped, however, that very soon we too, like my relatives, would be able to make good. Unfortunately, it has not worked out that way. For Francis, it was a major decision. He had not only to move out of his native village, but also to give up the vocation that he had been pursuing for almost 15 years. He was giving up a skilled, though not well paying, profession for an unskilled job.

Francis has been working for the same firm from the day we moved to Neendakara. With mechanisation of boats and the subsequent discovery of grounds for catching prawns, the accent in fishing has shifted altogether from fishing for domestic consumption to fishing for export, as far as the Neendakara area is concerned. The firm Francis works for exports prawns and squids, and has its own freezing plant.

Francis's job has been, from the outset, to sort out and grade the prawns according to the counts, pack them in cartons and load them into trucks. When he joined the firm in 1963, his daily wage was Rs. 2.50. In 1978, he was getting Rs. 10. Actually, this increase in 15 years works out to very little over one per cent per year. The workers' union is there and they made a lot of noise about wage increases, but you can judge for yourself from the experience of Francis what increases the union is actually able to get for the workers.

Francis has now given up his job altogether. For several months, he complained of pain in the joints, and therefore stayed at home. The Project hospital in Puthenthura is quite well staffed. But Francis did not have any faith in modern medicine. Allopathic cure is always temporary, he believes. He was going instead for a massage as prescribed by an Ayurvedic physician in the village. No doubt, he felt better as a result, but the moment he would go back to work his pain would reappear. That convinced him that his job gave him the pain. So he decided to give up the job. For several months, he was simply sitting at home doing nothing. That made him irritable also. For over a year now, he has been actively helping me in my prawn business and that has restored our domestic peace.

Our family

We have been married for over 20 years now. Three children, all girls, were born to me, the first one in Neendakara in my parents' house, with the help of a doctor sent home by the Project hospital. The other two were delivered in the government hospital in Quilon town. It is one of the oldest hospitals in the district, established as early as 1870. Nurses and midwives trained here have been staying for a long time in this village. Many families depend on them instead of going to the hospital. Since both my second and third children were Caesarean cases, the doctors advised me strongly to undergo hysterectomy. Francis and I did discuss the matter. It was a matter of my life and death, not of limiting the number of our children; at least, that is how we thought of the matter and came to the decision that the operation had to be undergone. So I underwent the operation after my third delivery. Still, both of us badly wanted a son. I cannot quite explain why we wanted a son. Maybe we fishermen are so conditioned since men go out to sea, never a woman. Did Francis want him more than I myself? Maybe I was more keen on it. We adopted a deserted infant through the hospital. He is now six years old. We call him Yesudas (which literally means the follower of Jesus), thus departing from the usual tradition of giving Latin names. Thus we now have four children, three girls and a boy.

Jacintha's college education

Jacintha, our eldest daughter, is now around 19 years old. Like me, she too is small in build. She has already completed her school and is in the fourth year at a college run by the church. She is studying for a degree in commerce. Educating her is, however, a major expense for us. Though the monthly college fee is only Rs. 15, we had to pay Rs. 200 as a special admission fee. Also, from the very beginning we had to put her in a private tutorial college. None of the regular colleges really prepare you well for examinations. The teachers themselves advise students to join tutorial classes. Some of these teachers run these tutorial classes in their off hours. Then there is the daily bus fare, which even at the concessional rates for students, adds up to some Rs. 12 a month. If you include expenses on books and clothing, the average works out easily to Rs. 100 a month.

Can we afford an expense of this order? Well, I would rather spend this much on my girl's higher education than build up savings for her dowry. In fact, I am certain that I won't be able to pay dowry at the going rates in our village. My worry, however, is that when the time for Jacintha's marriage comes, I may still be forced to give a big dowry. That will be ruinous. If Jacintha succeeds in getting a job after she completes her degree course, there is a good chance that she will be able to get married with less, if any dowry. Once you have a job, your income is counted as a part of the dowry; at least, this is what I am counting on.

Other children's education

Our 15-year old Mercy comes next. She is studying in the tenth standard in a high school in Sakthikulangara. Her education is virtually free in that there is very little to pay by way of tuition fee. Also, no expense for transportation is involved, but books and clothing are our responsibility. However, the cloth for the school uniform is available through the ration shop at a controlled price. Since Jacintha has no time for domestic chores, Mercy has to help me a great deal with chores like bringing water, cooking and cleaning.

Will Mercy too be sent to college? I am not so sure. She does not seem to be as interested in studies as Jacintha. Also, it will be difficult for me to have two children in college at the same time. It will be beyond my purse.

The third daughter, Agnes, is 13 years old. She is studying in the eighth standard at the upper primary school in Neendakara proper. Her education too is free. Agnes, though quite studious, also helps me a great deal with housework.

Yesudas, the six-year old adopted son, has also started going to the local school. The girls help him get ready for school and they look after him once they are back at home. Also, since my own parents live close by, he often goes there from school if no one is at home. Of course, now that Francis has no fixed schedule to observe any more, he is very often at home when the boy gets back from school. I myself have to be at the jetty on most days in the afternoon.

My work

I have been working ever since I was a child of eight or nine. I started as a shell collector. I would go to the beach along with my mother, carrying small nets to collect shells that are washed ashore with the breakers. My mother would sell the shells to merchants in the village and make a little money over and above what she made from vending fish. As I grew up, I was more and more involved in household chores for my mother. After marriage, however, I didn't take up outside work for quite some years. Only at the age of 28, i.e., seven years after my marriage, and some four years after we moved back to Neendakara with the family, did I decide to go to work.

Francis was not doing well and had started complaining about conditions of work in the factory. Also the family was much larger now and Francis's earnings were just not enough. Already, some women in the neighbouring households who earlier were either engaged in fish vending or doing only household chores, had started going out to the jetty to buy some catch, sort it out, peel the prawns, dry up the rest and then sell the whole thing for a small profit. I too gathered courage to take a plunge. I started going to the jetty with my sister Philomena to pick up the art. Soon I was fully involved.

Usually I go to the jetty at around noon. This is a convenient time for me. I cook a meal in the morning so that the children can eat and take food to school for their midday meal. The meal consists usually of rice and fish curry. After I myself have eaten I clean up the kitchen and leave for the jetty, locking up the house if Francis has other plans. Often, I wear a finely-checked neat *mundu,* wrapped on top of a petticoat and a cotton blouse on top of a bra. I carry a towel to cover my shoulders and wear rubber *chappals.* I also carry a small plastic purse to keep the vouchers from the firms to whom I sell prawns. While I tuck my cash into the top fold of my *mundu* at the waist, the vouchers are formal things to be kept separately.

Firms normally pay for the prawns they buy from the middlemen like myself on the following day or even later. Immediately on sale, all that I get is a voucher stating the quantity and grade of the material and the price which the firm will pay. So, the first thing I have to do when I set out for work is to call at the office of the firm concerned and claim my money.

It takes me one half to one hour to collect the cash that is owed to me. Then I head for the jetty.

I go to the jetty with my mother and sister. We wait there for the boats to come. As the boats land their catch, the auction starts instantly as the baskets are brought out. Cyclist merchants, all men from Quilon, and a few fish vending women from the neighbouring villages buy fish other than prawns. As for prawns, sometimes they are first sorted and then auctioned; sometimes they are sold without sorting. In either case, since the auction takes place on the basis of visual assessment, one has to have a very sharp eye and quick judgement in figuring out the grade and the weight of the prawns in a basket. You have to decide on the spot, within minutes of the landing of baskets, what final bid to make. One has also to form some judgement of the price the processed prawns will fetch from the exporting firms. The difficulty arises because the price fluctuates from day to day and quite widely, depending upon the extent of the overall catch during the day. The price can slump very fast on a day of a bumper catch. The difficulty of several middlewomen like me is that we have to be constantly guessing the price we will get for our processed product at the end of the day. Bigger middlemen carry less risk because they have usually a much more enduring relationship with the exporting firms.

Normally, all of us carry with us a couple of hundred rupees each in cash. But during the peak three months, we two sisters need not less than Rs. 1,500 together. Our mother only helps us with our work in organising and supervising things. Together, we may buy prawns for up to Rs. 2,500 on a peak day. Most boat owners know us and extend us overnight credit even though the general understanding at the auction is that all transactions are done in cash.

There are a number of jetties, but all are in Sakthikulangara, south of the highway bridge. Actually, the moment you cross the bridge, you are in Sakthikulangara. The jetty immediately to the west has 13 landing points, each privately owned and maintained. On the eastern side, most of the space along the bank of backwaters is taken up by the four largest fish exporting firms and the government. In the government boat yard, boats are made and repaired. On the private yards belonging to the four firms, the biggest boatyard is the one to which I have been going ever since I started going to work. This was a relatively neat yard and has plenty of space. But my principal reason for going there was that one of my second cousins was a major partner of the firm that owned this yard and, being a known party I got better treatment from the men around here.

The west-side boat jetty has the appearance very much of an Indian wholesale commodities market, with lots of people milling around in small knots. Each knot consists usually of persons bidding for one or more baskets of fish catch. There is always an auctioneer in their midst whose job it is to settle the bid. Very often, he is assisted by an assistant who notes down the various bids. The auctioneer and his assistant are employed by the jetty owners. At the end of each auction the auctioneer collects a fee of one per cent for the jetty owner. This is over and above the flat fee of Rs. 2 per boat every time it comes and berths at a jetty to unload. Every auction must be settled in cash. Therefore, a person who is participating in bidding must carry enough cash. Invariably the bidding starts with one rupee but it goes up quickly.

Every time a boat comes and stops in a jetty there is tremendous excitement. Immediately some baskets are handed over to the boat-hands who shovel the catch lying on the boat floor into these baskets with a spade and bring them out.

No sooner do the baskets full of fish appear than a few persons, men and women, gather around them. The catch is not always immediately auctioned. Sometimes, the boatmen might decide to have the catch first sorted out. There are always a number of women, young and old, wanting to work as sorters. In fact, there are too many of them, so the jetty staff have to shoo the extra ones away. The money each will get to do the sorting is always a paltry sum. At the end of a day, the lucky ones may have made as much as five rupees but most do not make more than four rupees. If a catch is auctioned without sorting, it is the buyer who gets the sorting done immediately thereafter at almost the same spot.

At the east-side boat jetty also, every basket of catch goes through the same motions of auction as on the west side. The place is far less crowded and also somewhat better organised. Boats that do not belong to the company owning the jetty are also allowed to berth here. The terms are the same as for boats berthing at the west side, but the turnover on the west side is much quicker.

I have been involved in the prawn business for over ten years now. I still vividly remember how I started my work by borrowing 100 rupees from friends and relatives. I participated in a number of auctions and made some profit. Since then I have never looked back. In the beginning, I would buy prawns and get some coolie to transport it home for me. The prawns were then peeled and cleaned and then placed in an iced basin. If the quantity of prawns was too much for the family (i.e., myself and my daughters) to peel, then I would call women from the neighbourhood to help me peel. Payment for peeling was, and is, made by the number of basins peeled. Each basin holds around two kilograms of peeled meat. It is always women and their children who did the peeling, and there was never any problem mobilising the number required even though peeling was done in the evenings. Gradually, as I bought larger and larger quantities I needed outside help with peeling more often.

During the lean periods, when the catch is small, the women who work for me come to borrow small amounts from me. These loans are given orally and carry no interest, but an obligation to peel for the lender as and when required. As the scale of my work expanded, we bought from the church two *cents* of land, next to my mother's hut, and put up a small peeling shed with an attached room. The peeling shed has a raised cement plastered floor with a slope so that the water gradually drains out on its own as the prawns are being peeled and cleaned. On one side is built a small circular trough, again cemented, for keeping the fish, if any, in the baskets.

After the prawns are peeled and cleaned, the meat, as it is called, is sold to one or the other of the prawn exporting firms. I take it to the firm's purchasing yard the same night, as soon as the peeling is finished. Since this is what everyone engaged in this business does, the exporting firms keep their purchasing booths open until quite late at night. The meat is graded and weighed immediately and a voucher issued to the seller for presentation the following morning for cash.

Investment in a second-hand boat

I have done reasonably well in my business of buying, processing and selling prawns. Whatever I earned was reinvested in my business. Since Francis was earning independently, I did not have to spend much out of my earnings on the family. A major part of my earnings could be put back in my business. Sometime in 1972, along with my youngest brother, Antony, who himself drives a mechanised boat, I purchased a second-hand boat, on a partnership basis. It was a 25-foot boat with a Bukh engine. Antony was supposed to operate the boat. Thus, while he would get both the 10 per cent share as the driver, and half of the 60 per cent belonging to the owner, I was to get only the owner's half. Both of us had to share the expenses on diesel and repairs equally. Unfortunately, however, the investment in the boat turned out to be a disaster. The boat has been in and out of the repair yard all these past eight years. We have spent no less than another Rs. 10,000 on repairs. Still the boat is not right. Today, I have a debt of Rs. 5,000 to repay.

My family

My father, 75-year old Joseph, is among the oldest residents of Neendakara. He is known as Joseph Moola as his house is a corner house. [*Moola* in Malayalam means a corner.] It is built here on a 10-*cent* piece of land which belonged to the church. He, like several others, was squatting here for several years. Then the church wanted him to vacate the land. While all the other families moved away, my father refused to oblige. He went to court and got his claim established to the piece of land. Now he has a comfortable three-room wooden house which is electrified. Also, it has all the necessary furniture such as cane seat chairs, one bed, one mirrored *almirah* and a couple of wooden stools. The house was done up when my youngest brother, Antony, the boat driver, was staying with our parents. Now he and his wife have set up a separate house of their own.

My father was an ordinary fisherman. He fished mostly with a cast net — a net that you may throw by the sweep of your arm standing at the bank of the sea. My mother, Thresia, now 65, was a fish vendor selling fish from door to door and at the Sakthikulangara fish market. Since both my father and mother belong to Neendakara, I have scores of relatives living in the village. I can count on my finger tips more than thirty first or second cousins. My parents are now quite old but in good health. They had ten children, five boys and five girls. My mother was married when she was 15 years of age. They lost two children as infants, both male children, and then a daughter when she was 48 years old. Now I have three brothers and four sisters alive. Both my parents come to the boat yard and take an active part in the business. All my brothers and sisters are living in the village and working. My brother Ben owns a workshop to repair boats. He went for a technical diploma. Another owns a small gill net boat with me. My other brother, Sebastian, is in the fish business on his own. My other sisters are also involved in prawn and fish work.

Running the house

When Francis was going to the factory he had to take one meal at the work site, but now that he is not going there anymore we take our morning meal together before I leave for my work. Francis comes to the jetty an hour or so later.

We have a ten unit ration card. I buy all the ration rice and sugar that we are entitled to. I find buying everyday a nuisance. Moreover, involved as I am in my business I do not have that much spare time for shopping. Of course, now Francis helps with major shopping. But I am the one who does whatever daily shopping, like buying of vegetables, tapioca and fish, has to be done.

I start the morning by making tea with milk and sugar. I buy milk from a nearby tea shop for 75 *paise* (one *paise* = one-hundredth of a rupee) in a steel container. We take tea in glass tumblers, which we keep in the cupboard when not in use. They break very easily if left on the floor and we cannot replace them often. I also make *puttu* (a mixture of rice flour and coconut kernel) and boil half a kilogram of green grams (pulses) as our breakfast. While the girls eat *puttu* at home they take rice and fish curry to school and college in their tiffin boxes. Since it is not certain what time I get back home from work, the evening meal has to be cooked by Agnes with the help of Mary. If Jacintha is back on time from her tutorial college, she too helps in cooking. The girls have quite a mutual understanding, so one does not notice much tension between them. Looking after little Yesudas is no problem either, particularly now, since Francis is usually around in the house.

Our daily earnings

I am unable to say what my average daily earnings are. How would you make an estimate of the daily earnings when business fluctuates so very wildly from day to day and from season to season? You have to remember that in Neendakara area the whole prawn business is virtually concentrated in two to three months of the rainy season. I can tell you this much, however, that but for my decision to start working, it would have been a hand-to-mouth existence even for our medium-sized family.

Maybe you can form some idea of our earnings from the expenses that we have to incur for our living. Though, as you can see, we live very modestly, our monthly expenses cannot be less than Rs. 500. When Francis had his factory job, he was able to contribute some Rs. 150 a month towards the family expenses. The balance was made up out of my earnings. In addition, it has been possible for me to get some small items of jewellery from time to time for our three daughters. Then there is this investment in land and a second-hand mechanised boat. Of course, since the land prices have gone up fast in recent years, my investment in land has proven to be wise. But I doubt that our mechanised boat, in which Antony and I have together sunk some Rs. 20,000, will fetch more than half that sum. That has turned out to be a major mistake. I also require a working capital of Rs. 1,000 to transact my daily business. Still, the debt I have to repay is only Rs. 5,000.

116

Looking ahead

The mechanisation of boats and the discovery of prawn in Neendakara sea did not benefit the women directly because we women do not go out to sea for fishing. Some people might, as you say, even complain that the Project, as such, completely ignored women. But I am not really worried about whether they thought of men first and women later. The fact remains that for women not only from within the Project villages, but also from outside, immense new work possibilities were thrown open. Take my own case; but for the Project, I would have been like one of those headload fish vendors you see in other towns and villages eking out a miserable living. I have no doubt that even a family of such modest means as ours can think of our future with some confidence only because of the Project. Maybe many have become very rich, but even we have become better off than before.

RAMANI

The net maker

Name	RAMANI	No. of children lost under five years of age	Three
Village	Puthenthura		
Age	56	Family planning status	Hysterectomy at age 41 when last child was five
Education	Went to school for some years	Occupation	Making fishing nets
Age at marriage	22	Husband's occupation	Fishing, using a large traditional craft
Dowry	Nil		
No. of pregnancies	Five (only two sons survive)	Ownership	Owns no craft
No. of births in hospital	One (last)	Type of house	Thatched hut and squatting on government land
No. of births at home	Four		

We live, as you can see, very close to the sea-shore in Puthenthura. The sea is just a few minutes' walk from our hut. The open air stage in front of our hut was built by a local group for the villagers to stage plays on festive occasions. We have been living here for the last 25 years and have grown to like the location of our hut. That is why we did not apply for the allotment of one of the new brick houses put up by the government on the east side. We are hoping that the government will allot to us some ten *cents* of land right where we are squatting. After a hundred families have moved out from this west side, it has considerably eased the congestion and we have started liking it here even better.

Present occupants of the hut

In this small hut, my 61-year old husband, Raman, and I live with our second unmarried son, Dharm, who is 20 years old. Our older son, who is married, lives separately with his wife in the adjacent hut. Though Raman is virtually illiterate, having been at school only for two years, he is still called Asan by everyone in this village. *Asan* in Malayalam means teacher. He is referred to as such because he is not only a good fisherman but also one who is ready to share his knowledge of the sea and the movements of the fish shoals with others. He is so very adept at fishing that he seldom comes back without fish when he is at sea. So everyone, young or old, asks him when and where to go fishing. Our hut has been the meeting place for young fishermen. This in a way is of great help as we can mobilise a crew at short notice.

Being Raman's wife, they call me Asati (which mean a teacher's wife in Malayalam). I have been at school longer than Raman and have studied until the fifth standard. So I can read and write well. I was particularly good at math and even now I often help Asan with his calculations. After our craft comes back from the sea, the auction proceeds from the day's catch are shared by all the crew members in our verandah. I am always around to help them out with their arithmetic.

Raman's work

Though Raman is now past 60, he is still quite active. He takes out his craft, a *thanguvallom,* to sea on as many days as he can. In this village, two kinds of craft are mostly used. *Thanguvallom,* a large plank-built boat and *kochuvallom,* a smaller boat. The *thanguvallom* is a 40-foot long canoe. Its planks are tied together with coir ropes which pass through various holes made for this purpose in the planks and then nailed together with copper nails which don't rust. The holes and joints are filled in with substances that do not dissolve in water. *Thanguvallom* takes a crew of nine to eleven persons and operates a type of local purse-seine net called *thanguvala.* Ordinarily, a *thanguvallom* is operated from the middle of July to the end of September. Since we do not own a *kochuvallom,* Raman takes the *thanguvallom* practically all through the year except during the months when it is utterly dangerous to go out to sea. *Kochuvallom* is a smaller but more versatile craft which needs a crew of four to five persons. So far we have never owned one.

Raman has a regular crew of nine young men. This includes our older son and a few relatives. Though we own only one net, it is quite a versatile type capable of hauling all kinds of fish. The cost of a new net is some Rs. 15,000. It is made of white nylon twine. Most of the men who work for us belong to this village and are related to us either through blood or marriage. Raman usually goes out in the morning and spends some six hours fishing. It takes them approximately one to one and a half hours to reach the fishing grounds. They have to reach a certain depth before they can spot the shoals. Coming back to the shore usually takes less time. The catch is auctioned off as soon as it is landed and is paid for in cash on the spot. Raman and his men sit down in our verandah to distribute the cash. We get two out of eleven shares, one for our craft and one for Raman as a crew member. The nine crew members, including Gyan, get one share each.

Engine for a traditional craft

Recently a well known engineering company, which manufactures marine engines of Japanese design, offered to fit an outboard engine temporarily to our craft to demonstrate how a traditional craft itself can be mechanised. Raman is quite impressed with the engine because the craft can make a trip faster with less physical strain, though the size of the crew remains the same. The use of the engine will mean that the crew will have more time and energy to fish. But it will reduce the life of the boat because of the vibration and also involve increased maintenance costs. If we can raise a bank loan, we still intend to buy the engine. As you know, the banks give loans to

119

fishermen on concessional terms. The local agent of the manufacturing company is confident that our local bank will give us the loan for buying the engine.

Sending a son to the Gulf

We could have raised funds for this engine from other sources as well if we were not already in debt. Our younger son, Dharm, has been very interested in going to the Gulf. Twenty years old, he has finished ten years of his schooling. He appeared twice for the school-leaving certificate examination, but could not pass it. English language was his weak point. This is the case with most of the children here. We were hoping to send him to college. Since going to college was out of the question, he went on to a technical training school for a diploma course in fibre moulding. This school, run by the government, was located some 20 kilometres away from our village. That is how we could manage to change his profession. We are fed up with this uncertain and hand-to-mouth existence. I would like my children at least to have a steady income. I don't care if they have to give up fishing. After finishing the course, Dharm could have gone for a more advanced course in Madras, but before we could decide on that we met an agent from Quilon who came looking for young men willing to go to the Gulf. In recent years, quite a few young men from our own village have gone to the Gulf. I know all of their names. They are the talk of the village because their families have become suddenly rich. I never thought that either of our sons would make it to the Gulf. When the agent from Quilon suggested that Dharm would make it, if we raised the necessary money, I jumped at the idea. The agent feels that with his education and technical training he will get for Dharm a contract as part of a group of some fifty men required by an Italian furniture making firm in Abu Dhabi. According to him 20 out of 50 persons already enrolled for this contract are from Kerala State.

His job will carry pay of Rs. 2,000 plus board and lodging. Usually people going to the Gulf can send back more than two-thirds of the cash salary for which they are hired there. So the debt one incurs to send young men to the Gulf is possible to clear within 16 to 18 months. Then one can think in terms of improvements in one's working and living condition.

Raising the money

The first thing to do however was to raise the sum of Rs. 13,000. This would cover not only the premium payable to the agency for arranging the job and immigration clearance (normally we refer to this as the NOC, meaning no-objection certificate), but also the one-way air ticket which costs Rs. 3,442. Immediately, I offered to give away whatever gold I had accumulated over the years from my earnings from net making. Savings from fishing are always used up in replacing the craft and net, though, over the years, our craft and equipment both have become not only better, but more expensive. The nylon net Raman uses is quite expensive. Also, his *thanguvallom* is only two years old. But there was no question of selling or mortgaging our craft and gear. By pooling together my gold and my daughter-in-law's, I could raise Rs. 4,500. For the rest of the money, I had to go around and ask all our friends and relatives to give cash or a gold bangle or two, to be pledged for cash, on the clear understanding that each of them would be paid back as soon as the son starts sending money from the Gulf. The money was not difficult to raise. People in the village are now used to contributing their mite for this purpose. I do not know of a single case in our village where money thus raised has not been paid back. We have deposited the full amount with the agent. Dharm has already received his passport and is now waiting to be called any day.

We are keeping our fingers crossed. We hope very much that once Dharm makes it, he will work out some way of getting his elder brother, Gyan, also to the Gulf.

My childless daughter-in-law

Gyan is now 34 years old. He went to school for nine years. Thereafter, he joined his father's crew. When he was 25, we got him married. We got a dowry of Rs. 1,000 and 70 grams of gold. We used the cash to make a payment for the new craft that we were negotiating for. In fact I asked my daughter-in-law to give also part of her gold jewellery. This was one of the causes of misunderstanding between us. We have not been able to return her cash and gold so far. Recently, when she saw that we needed money for Dharm, she went and left with her mother whatever gold jewellery she had. Apart from this, there is another important reason for misunderstanding between my daughter-in-law and myself. I have been urging my son to send his wife away because she has not borne him any child in ten years. We have taken her for treatment to all types of doctors and hospitals. Thrice she has undergone curetage. Even my son has been tested for his virility (sperm count). He has been found normal. Evidently, something is terribly wrong with her. But my son does not agree that we should send his wife back to her parents. Instead, they are looking for a child to adopt. I do not like that idea but I cannot force my ideas on him beyond a point.

Daughter-in-law sets up a separate house

For the first eight years, Gyan and his wife were staying with us in this hut. My daughter-in-law would do all the kitchen work and I could make the nets. Then once we had a big row and I gave her a couple of slaps. She was in her period, according to us in a polluted state, and absent-mindedly touched certain things. Maybe I overdid it but she was getting on my nerves too much. In spite of her being childless, she was lazy and complaining. Also, I was never very happy with the way she was doing her domestic chores. One day this break had to happen. Moreover, she wanted Gyan to give her his share of the money he earned. Then they decided to move away. Gyan with the help of his father erected a small hut close to ours. I see very little of my daughter-in-law these days; we are still not on talking terms.

My own work

I have been working since I got married and went to Raman's village to live with him. I would defibre coir husks and make cotton nets. The use of nylon threads had not appeared on the scene and nets were made only with cotton threads. But ever since

121

we moved to Puthenthura I have been engaged in making nylon trawl nets and trying to keep the money for special purposes. Sometimes I buy a little gold item.

There are two net dealers in our village. Both of them deal in trawl nets. They buy nylon twine in bulk and farm it out in small lots to the women working for them. I work for the dealer who has some 60 to 70 women, young and old, from our village working for him. These are all women who, for one reason or other, have to stay at home. The dealer keeps getting orders all the time for trawl nets. Each mechanised boat has at least two trawl nets and they wear out in a short while. So there is always demand for them. I collect the twine from the net dealer's house. His wife is there always. She also gives instructions regarding the sections of the net to be knitted. Indeed, she is the one who weighs the twine and keeps an account of it. When we return the knitted sections to her, she weighs them again. One gets paid for knitting on the basis of weight, but the payment is small compared to what one can earn in jobs outside one's house.

I do all my knitting in our verandah. I know the mesh size and the number of knots that are necessary to start with and then taper off for each portion of the net. There are seven distinct parts of the trawl net. To assemble each part, one has to do several sections. For instance, to do the main face, you need four panels, each starting with 400 meshes and ending up with 300.

Time disposition

I get up around 5 o'clock in the morning. It has become a habit over the years. Even if I want to sleep longer, I cannot. The first thing I do is to brush my teeth and have a wash. I have a nice enclosed area at the back of our house where I can have a wash and then I go to the seaside tea shop. There are twelve shops but I go to the one very close to the sea-shore run by a woman. Once I get back home I clean the front yard and say my prayers. By then it is clear daylight, so I sit down for net making. Around 9 a.m. I make some breakfast for myself. Usually, this is leftover rice and gruel from the previous night. Then I must take a break and do my shopping. My morning shopping consists of firewood and spices. There are two fuel shops and six grocery shops in the village. There are, in addition to the two ration shops, some twelve women who sell just rice. We need to buy extra rice because the ration quota is never adequate. But I buy all the rice, sugar and kerosene I am entitled to by our ration card from the ration shop to which we are assigned. I cook rice only once for both the meals. I make a fish curry every day. Sometimes, I also make a coconut chutney. Grinding spices for the fish curry is the main chore. Raman and Dharm eat their meals at home but separately. It is only for the evening meal that we are always together. In the afternoon, first I feed both the men and then have my own meal. The vessels have to be washed and leftover rice and gruel stored away for the evening. In the afternoon, I take a little break before getting back to net making. In between work, when I feel like taking tea, I go to the tea shop. A little before dusk, around 6:30 in the afternoon, I clean the prayer room and sweep the yard. The two brass lamps have to be scrubbed and cleaned every day before they are lighted for evening prayers. After this, I can put in some more work in the evenings because Raman spends an hour or two at the toddy shop. All told, I am able to devote six to eight hours a day to net making, but I seldom make more than four rupees a day. Of course, we do not get paid on a daily basis.

I am now used to Raman's drinking. I have learned to take these things in my stride the hard way. When I was young, I would protest strongly and get beaten up in the process. His drinking was the only matter on which there used to be a problem between us. Otherwise, he was always ready to leave quite a lot for me to handle. I am therefore very deeply involved in matters connected with his work. As I have told you already, I help Raman with accounts and other matters connected with fishing. His crew members and others who have dealings with him have become accustomed to my involvement.

Early background

I was born and bred in this very village; so were both my parents. My mother, who lived until the ripe age of 80, died only recently. My father owned two crafts, the big and the small one, and the nets to go with them, while my mother was a midwife. She made some money by attending women's deliveries. For every delivery she attended she would get a new set of clothes and some cash depending on the household and the sex of the child.

My parents had eight children in all. Of these, two, both female, died in infancy. Of the six surviving children, four were boys and two girls. Except for my younger sister, Radha who is married outside the village, the rest of us live in Puthenthura. All of us were sent to school for some years. My youngest brother studied until the tenth standard. He is the only one working on a mechanised craft. He goes to the neighbouring village of Sakthikulangara on most days. When it is off-season he travels to the northern part of the state, going as far as Cannanore with the boat. Then he has to stay away from home for several days at a stretch. My other three brothers are engaged in traditional fishing, each owning his own craft and gear and living separately with his own family in this very village.

My marriage

I was married in 1947 at the age of 22 to Raman from the neighbouring village of Kureepuzha. Raman was 28 years old. Our families knew each other, being distantly related. They came to ask for me and once the arrangement was agreed upon, we got married. The Araya priest conducted the ceremony. Raman's people gave me a new set of clothes. I had to change into those clothes before departing for their house. There was no exchange of dowry. Kureepuzha was a village where coir defibring and spinning was one of the mainstays of the people. When I went there, I too started defibring husks. Raman's parents had five surviving children. Two had died, one male and one female. Raman was their second of the surviving sons. His father had a share in a *thanguvallom* along with six others, but he owned a *kochuvallom* all by himself. We stayed there with them for four years. Raman worked for his father at that time. In the fifth year, we moved to another village where Raman bought a piece of land.

Children

Of the five children I gave birth to, only two, both sons, have survived. The other three were girls. I was expecting my first child within a year. I came away to Puthenthura to my parents when I was five months pregnant, according to our custom. My mother and other relatives helped me with my confinement. The baby, a boy, was delivered at home and I was taken care of in the traditional way. This meant having a hot water bath after an oil massage and taking herbal tonics. My parents, particularly my father, were strong believers in the Ayurvedic tradition. Most people in the village know the recipes and often make them at home. There are other medicines that you have to buy from Ayurvedic medicine shops. I went back to Raman's village only when the child was three months. Most Araya parents try to keep the couple apart for some time before and after childbirth. The practice is wearing out these days because when girls go to hospitals for delivery they don't spend much time with their own parents. Very often girls married to boys of Puthenthura don't even go back. It is not good for their health to be together so soon after childbirth. I did not get the boy vaccinated. Instead I just kept giving him a herbal mixture which was supposed to protect him from all virus infections. The child was breastfed for three years until I was expecting my second child. My second child was a girl. The girl was growing up nicely. When she was five years old she was drowned in the backwaters. In between, I had another child, again female. She lived for two and a half years only and died after an intestinal infection. My fourth child again was a girl who lived for only one year. She had developed a breathing problem and she died before we could get her to a hospital. Losing three children within a period of three years or so was a big shock to us. I was feeling very depressed. Rightly or wrongly, I did not feel like staying any more in Kureepuzha. I wanted to go back to Puthenthura. Raman agreed to the move for my sake, but only on an experimental basis. At that time, Puthenthura was more advanced than Kureepuzha, thanks largely to the Project. The Project hospital was situated next door. Also, the villagers were given easy access to safe drinking water. Not that Raman was worried about making good as a fisherman, because he was already an expert in traditional fishing, but there is always uncertainty about moving to a new place of work, away from your own friends and relations. Anyway, the move to Puthenthura proved to be permanent.

In Puthenthura, I felt more secure. I was now close to my parents. But having been left with just one son was a source of constant anxiety. My anxiety became greater and greater with the passage of time as I did not conceive again. So I was advised to undertake weekly fasts and I made rounds of various temples. I conceived Dharm, my second son, after a five-year interval. This was in 1960. My mother was still living, but she had become too old to help me deliver at home. So, unlike my first four deliveries, it was decided that I should go for my fifth delivery to the Project hospital, which was located just next door to where we had put up our hut. The hospital staff insisted on vaccinating the baby. So my second son has gone through the whole course. I breastfed all my children, but I fed the last one for five years because I did not conceive thereafter. In 1965, my uterus had to be removed because of some complications.

Looking ahead

Looking back, I feel we have worked very hard and tried our best to bring up the two boys to the best of our abilities. I myself have not wasted a single day in my life. All the money that I got from making nets, little though it was always, went towards educating the boys. True, I have used up part of the dowry brought by my daughter-in-law, but I am not at all ashamed on that score. We used it for the good of the family, and that includes her as well.

The people in the village feel I am lucky since I have sons only, but I am not so sure of that. In old age, a daughter can be of greater help. A son, however nice and obedient, will never help you with the household chores. And unless you are very lucky, it is hard to get loyalty and affection from a daughter-in-law. She is always wanting to sow the seeds of separation between a mother and her son. I believe if a joint family has to survive, a daughter-in-law must be kept in firm control. We have become too lenient these days.

Ideally, if both of our sons can go to the Gulf to work, we should be able to build a good house. Also, we could build up enough savings to take care of ourselves during our old age. My younger son has promised that he will not let us down. I am not so sure of the elder son. He is good, but his wife can prevail on him to do things differently. All the same, we have to be concerned about him as much as about our unmarried son.

SARLA

The chit fund operator

Name	SARLA	No. of children lost under five years of age	None
Village	Puthenthura		
Age	35	Family planning status	Had sterilisation after fifth child
Education	Studied until the ninth standard	Occupation	Chitty business and running tea shop
Age at marriage	19	Husband's occupation	Coolie fisherman
Dowry	Nil	Ownership status	Owns a large traditional craft and a seine net
No. of pregnancies	Five		
No. of births in hospital	Five	Type of house	Owns a house with 480 sq. ft. and asbestos roof constructed and given for fishermen by government, has defaulted on monthly dues
No. of births at home	None		

I was born in the neighbouring fishing village of Chirayinkil in 1946. Though both my parents are living, they are separated. My mother lives with my younger brother very close to where I live now in Puthenthura, whereas my father continues to live, as always, with his second wife and their children in Chirayinkil. My mother, who has been in indifferent health practically all her life, is still working. She works as a part-time sweeper in a sea food exporting firm in the neighbouring village of Neendakara for a monthly salary of Rs. 35. It is a small amount no doubt, but she gets it regularly, month after month, and that means a lot to poor people like us.

Early separation of my parents

When my mother was around 16 years of age, her father got her married into a family that was reasonably well off and well known to him. It was nearly an alliance between the two Araya families. One had land and money and the other, that is, my mother's family, was better educated and known for Sanskrit learning and knowledge of Ayurvedic medicine. Dowry was there even then, but not as large as it is today. She was given a sum of Rs. 300 in cash as dowry. Her wedding was performed by the Araya Service Organisation.

Although my mother had been to school for 4 to 5 years, she was neither healthy nor good looking. It appears that right from the very start she did not hit it off with either my father's parents, especially his mother, or my father himself. On top of that, the first two children born to her were female. The first one was stillborn and the second, born within one year of the first, was myself. The story is that, after her second delivery at her parents' house, when my mother returned to my father's house along with me as an infant, she found herself most unwelcome. My father's people spread the word that an astrologer had predicted that my mother would bear him only seven daughters and no son. They felt that this would amount to a total disaster for the household. They would not only have to find seven bridegrooms, but also mobilise seven dowries. So they wanted my mother to leave their house along with her child, so that my father could marry another woman. My mother refused to oblige however, without a proper settlement which took time to work out. She had a tough time there, having to stay put in a completely hostile environment day after day, but she stuck to her guns.

The settlement between my parents

Since their marriage had been registered with the local caste service association, the Araya Samithi, the dispute between my parents had to go to the association. A settlement was reached whereby my father was made to repay the dowry money, raise and educate me until the age of 16 and then get me married and pay my mother a sum of Rs. 7 every month towards her maintenance. By the time all this was sorted out, I had reached the age of five.

My up-bringing

I grew up with my father and step-mother thereafter. My mother, who had moved back to her parents' house, would come to see me occasionally and take me with her during summer breaks from school. I stayed in school until I reached the ninth standard. The school was a good one hour's walk from where we lived, but my step-mother always wanted me to complete all the housework she had assigned to me before leaving for school. This meant drawing water from the well, cleaning the yard and the house, and washing my step-brothers and step-sisters. My step-mother never quite liked the idea of my going to school. She was always asking my father to keep me back so that I could help her. However, better sense prevailed and since I wanted so much to go to school, my father allowed me to continue. I enjoyed school though it meant walking long distances. I had my girl friends and also it was a respite from home. When I completed my ninth standard, I felt I had had enough of my step-mother. I decided to move in with my mother who was by then living with her little son born to her outside of wedlock in Puthenthura.

My mother's affair and pregnancy

Though my mother was staying with her brothers in Chirayinkil, she used to travel to Puthenthura to visit her elder sister who was living there with her husband and their children. She earned her keep by defibring coir husks. She had kept the dowry money that was returned by my father with her brother to be re-invested as a loan so that it could earn her some interest. With the passage of years, there arose some misunderstanding between brother and sister about the money he was keeping for her. In this matter, my mother's sister's husband played quite a role. I think this was his way of gaining my mother's confidence and getting closer to her. This resulted in a relationship between the two and ended up in my mother conceiving from him. That came as a great shock to everyone including her own sister. I was around 13 years of age then and could understand what had happened. The two sisters had a big quarrel and my mother was thrown out of their house. She decided to put up a thatched hut in Puthenthura itself with the help of some village men. She also started looking for work there. This was sometime in 1958. With the introduction of mechanised boats under the Norwegian Project, trawling for prawns had already started paying dividends. My mother found work as a peeler with a prawn exporting firm in the next village. She had to walk the three kilometre distance.

My mother's hut was next door to this small Project hospital. Therefore, having a child without the help of relatives and at such a late age did not pose a big problem for my mother. The new hospital next door, though small, was well equipped. It was specially geared to look after the needs of women and children. She had her confinement there. I now had a brother who was 13 years younger than me. Though I felt somewhat embarrassed about it in the beginning, I still felt drawn more to my own mother's child than to my step-mother's children. My mother had to resume working soon after her delivery and needed my help. I decided therefore to give up my studies and move to Puthenthura. Though my father was not quite happy about it, I think my step-mother persuaded him not to prevent me.

My marriage to Soman

After I moved to Puthenthura with my mother, my main preoccupation was to look after my kid brother and attend to the household chores, while my mother was away at work. Thus, I stayed mostly at home, keeping fully occupied with domestic chores. Soman, a young coolie fisherman of the same village working on a traditional craft, would often pass by our hut on his way to the coast. He had lost his father when he was around 12 years old. His father had some serious throat infection and was sick for six months. They had to spend quite a lot of money on his treatment. Soman stayed in school only for three years and ever since then has been helping his family. Once his father died, his responsibilities increased. He had three older sisters who had to be married off. They sold their seven *cents* of land and got the girls married in the neighbouring fishing villages and moved to squat on government land. They also had to borrow money, so his mother was steeped in debt. Her hope was that Soman's wife would bring a good dowry so that she could pay up part, if not all, of her debt. However, as time passed, Soman and I got to know each other and developed an attachment. We both started toying with the idea of getting married to each other. My mother had noticed the development of our relationship and was not opposed to the idea of our getting married. People were talking about our interest in each other and the gossip reached my father. But when my father heard about it, he stoutly rejected it saying, 'I haven't brought up this girl to marry an illiterate coolie fisherman'. He came personally and threatened Soman that if he saw me any more he would face grave consequences. At this turn of events, I was so severely dejected that one day I decided to end my life and threw myself into the sea, but I was pulled out in time by some men, who had been suspicious of my movements. That is when my mother made up her mind to go ahead and get me married to Soman without delay. At a simple wedding ceremony, Soman gave me a new set of clothes and we were married. My father must have felt great anger at the news of our marriage but the only way he showed his displeasure was not to contact me ever since then. Nor have I tried to make contact with him and his family.

Our children

We have been married for 16 years now. We have five children, three girls and two boys. I went to the Project hospital for nearly all my confinements. Very good care is taken there, before and after delivery, of the mother as well as children. I wanted to go in for sterilisation after my third child when I got a son, but both my mother and Soman would not hear of it. Several of my friends and neighbours had been sterilised already and there were not many who complained about the side-effects of the operation. Somehow, both Soman and my mother feared that I would become a permanent invalid as a result. Using alternative methods of family planning never even cropped up. No one to my knowledge in the village even considers them seriously, though doctors and nurses in the hospital do talk about them often.

Whenever I complained about the size of the family, my mother would console me that she was always there to render her services. It is true that she was one person I could always depend on, though she was an invalid all her life. Soman and Yogi, my brother, have always helped with the children by taking them out and playing with them. Still the major task of feeding, clothing, cleaning and doing the lessons really fell on me more than anyone else. By the time I could persuade them to let me have an operation, I had two more children. I felt I had more than I could really take care of. There were three other women who were also anxious to have their tubes tied and we decided we should go together and we gave each other moral support. Seeing that I was determined, Soman and my mother agreed. The doctors were more than willing to do the operation as I had four children and was expecting the fifth. I am glad that I do not have to go through any more pregnancies. I keep so busy that I am waiting even for my young one to start regular school.

All my children are in school except the youngest who is just three years old. I send him to a nursery called Anganwadi, run by the government, where he gets even a midday meal. My 14-year old daughter, the eldest, has reached the ninth standard. The other two children are in the sixth and fifth standard. I plan to keep them in school as long as they show interest. So far, they have been fairly serious, so it might be easier for them to stay on. Until recently, the nearest high school was four kilometres distant. Children from our village would walk to and from the school in all seasons. Parents have been particularly reluctant to send grown-up girls. Now that we have a high school in our village, this has made education for our children more accessible. In this respect Sakthikulangara is more fortunate because the church there has all along been taking a lead in establishing schools.

Soman's work

When I got married, Soman was just a coolie fisherman, so he made a very modest living. We also had Soman's mother to care of as her health was quickly deteriorating. She was in an anaemic condition and this persisted; she passed away in 1968 after only four years of our marriage.

There were days on which Soman made no money whatsoever. But in season he made good money, something like Rs. 10 to Rs. 15. Since he was not addicted to drink, he would bring back practically all the money he made. But we could barely manage.

I start my chitty business

Soon after I got married, I felt I had to work and earn and contribute to the family pool. Since Soman did not own any craft or gear, he had to look for work every day. With his mother heavily indebted, he was obliged to work for the persons who had lent them money. This also meant that he got work only on days when fishermen with crafts needed extra hands to work for them. During the peak seasons for fishing, of course, there was no problem in getting work, but whatever he got by way of his share was not adequate. During the lean seasons when the sea was rough, things could be difficult. In any case, it appeared that he would never be able to extricate himself from his mother's indebtedness.

I was quite educated, more than most other fisherwomen of my age. Also, I knew a little about running a chit fund, which is really a mutual savings club, from my father. I also had some experience in running a chit fund even at school. Children would get together and pool their money and take turns in buying their basic requirements. I thought of starting a chit fund for women in the village. The idea was that a number of women would contribute Rs. 2.50 every week so that each member would have saved Rs. 100 in ten months. Most women in our village were making a few rupees from weaving nets. In virtually all fishing households here in these villages women are engaged in making nets. The money they earn is kept strictly for their own personal use. Men seldom lay claim to it, though they may like to know how much they make. Most men are themselves members of one chitty or the other. That is how they raise funds needed for repairing the craft or replacing the roof or meeting some other major expense. So there was no question of opposition from men to the idea of women joining a chitty out of their own earnings. To start with, nine women agreed to join my first chitty. I was the tenth member. At the end of every month, I got together these members to decide by auction who would get the amount of Rs. 100 they had put together in the chitty. The auction is about the amount a member is willing to surrender in lieu of the right to have the lump sum. The amount surrendered in the first auction was as high as 30 rupees. Each of these nine women members had to pay only Rs. 22 for the month. My commission as an organiser was five per cent of the amount collected every month. In addition, I was actually entitled to take the first month's collection as a loan without surrendering any portion thereof on auction. But to start with I let the other members bid for the first month's collection and on the occasions I did not require the money, I could auction it and the surrender money would belong to me in full. I got five rupees out of this as my remuneration and the balance of

25 rupees was to be distributed among the nine members other than the member who took the principal by way of reduced contribution in the month that had just started. The problem was not keeping accounts but collecting the money from members. Often, I would have to visit them at home. In time, I found out when each of my members was most likely to have the money to pay up her contribution. I kept the accounts neatly and carefully and read them out to the members at the time of the auction. Within a few months I was approached by other women for membership. So I started a second chitty. After a year or so, some women who, like my mother, were peeling prawns wanted me to have a chitty where they could put in Rs. 50 per month for a 20-month period. Though I started this business in a very modest way, with the faith and confidence I was able to build up, I have now a steady income of Rs. 80–100 per month. I manage four to five chitties at any one time.

Move to the government housing colony

It was around 1968 that the Kerala State Government decided to construct some 100 houses to the east of the highway passing through Puthenthura. The houses were meant for fishermen living on the west side squatting on government land. The houses were to be laid out properly around a backwater canal. They would be made with burnt bricks and cement mortar and have an asbestos roofing. Each house would be independent with an access of its own and with a drinking water tap within easy reach. Though each house was to cost the government Rs. 8,000, those who would be allotted the house had to pay only Rs. 4,000 and that too in instalments of Rs. 25 per month. One could get an electric connection by paying some extra money. To be eligible for allotment you would have to show that you did not own any land. Soman applied for one of these houses along with some 20 others from the west side. I had been all along hoping that we would get an allotment and was very happy to move to the new home in 1978.

The house

The house has, as you can see, a built-in area of 480 square feet, with a little open area around it that you can call your own. We have two proper rooms, a kitchen and a verandah. Though the accommodation available to us is infinitely better than what anyone had on the west side, people's expectations from the government were very much higher. You can hear practically every one of us complain that the walls are not cement plastered, the doors are not good, and the roofing could have been better. I know that the house would then have cost a lot more and I am not sure we could have paid more by way of monthly instalments. In fact, most of us have defaulted on our instalments and very few of us pay any attention to the notices of outstanding dues that we receive regularly from the government, hoping that one day the government will agree to write off our dues.

131

A tea shop for women and children

About one year back, after we moved to our new house, I got the idea of running a small tea shop. I always had some surplus cash, so I decided to start a small tea shop for serving morning tea, coffee and snacks to women and children. Since quite a few women from our village go to the neighbouring villages for peeling work, they tend to go out for their morning tea and snacks. In ordinary tea shops in this village, there is no separate place for women to sit, so they take their tea and snacks standing. I thought my tea shop would permit them to have their tea and snacks in a much more comfortable way, and I must say that my idea has worked well. Running a tea shop, I must admit, is not considered a very respectable occupation. Since an ordinary tea shop is on a roadside and caters to a wide variety of men, it would be difficult for young women to handle it. You not only have to serve tea but have to make conversation with everyone. Since I am running my tea shop for only women and children around here, these problems don't crop up. Since my mother works only part-time because of her indifferent health and as she stays so close to our home, she helps me with my tea shop as often as she can. For the tea shop, I have put up another thatched room next to our kitchen. Here I not only store firewood but also do all the pounding and grinding work required for the snacks that I cook to go with tea and coffee. I have collected grinding and pounding stones and built a platform three feet above the ground where all the cooking is done. In our small verandah we have kept a long table and a bench to go with it for use by my customers. My major investment was in the thatched room, furniture and additional cooking utensils. The amount I needed for the purpose added up to Rs. 100. The idea was to stretch whatever we had and then slowly buy the other things. My daily profit from the tea shop comes to 6 to 8 rupees. You cannot call this profit because I have to put in a lot of hard work. Moreover, Yogi and my mother also help me a great deal and they only get breakfast in return. The main difference between me and women who go out to work for others is that I make the same amount of money working at home.

Time schedule

From the day I started the tea shop, I have had to get up before 4 o'clock in the morning. When my mother feels up to it, she comes over to help me with such work that is not so heavy. I get my breakfast ready. Once the snacks are halfway ready, I then get the huge pan of water to boil. Around 5 to 5:30 a.m., both tea and snacks are ready. Then the children have to be awakened and made to have a wash so they can go to school. My mother is of great help to me. Apart from the help in the kitchen, she gets the children ready for school. Also, Soman and my brother are taken care of by her. Of course, they are not there on days when they have gone to sea in the early hours of the morning. My 14-year old daughter also lends me her hand but I want her to devote as much of her time as possible to her studies. I want very much that she completes her school well. If she does well, I shall be happy to send her to college; then she may be able to get a steady job or some government service. But I don't wish to think big. It often ends up in disappointment. At the same time I would like her to become something good before she thinks of marriage.

The customers start coming at about 7 o'clock in the morning. I can usually wind up things by 10 o'clock in the morning. Cleaning of the vessels and the place easily takes an hour thereafter. I need another one hour to do the daily washing. Then I put rice on a slow fire to cook and go out to do the daily shopping.

Also I have to collect the chitty dues from women who have not yet paid up. I sit down to write up my tea shop accounts before or after lunch depending upon when I get back home from shopping. I take a little nap if there is time. Soman and Yogi take lunch at home. Then it is time for the children to get back from school and they have to be fed and washed. If necessary, I go out for an hour or so to look up my clients or do the shopping that could not be done before noon. Then the brass prayer lamp has to be washed and lit so that we all can say the evening prayer. My mother is there to get the children ready for this. In my house I see to it that we have dinner early so that the vessels can be rinsed and we can retire not too late. This helps me get up early enough to start the morning. So, you can see how busy I am during all my waking hours.

A few items of furniture, the one-band radio, and the time piece you see in our house were bought one by one over the years. The amount I can draw from the chitties I run has been very handy whenever we had to incur a major expense. However, the most important item we have been able to buy with the help of the chitties is the *vallom,* the big traditional craft and its gear known by the name *kambavala*; though second-hand, it meant a tidy sum which we paid up over a period.

Soman now does not have to go fishing as a coolie. He can hire people now. Yogi, my 24-year old brother, works with Soman on the same craft. If there is one single achievement in our lives that I feel proud of, it is that Soman now owns a craft of his own, and that too a *thanguvallom* and a *kambavala*.

Looking ahead

When I look back at my life, you can certainly say that I have come a long way. Though as a child I got little affection from my parents, still I had access to steady education. This proved to be a great asset. I married the man of my own choice, to the great discomfiture of my father, with the result that he gave me up altogether. I had very little contact even with my other relatives, who virtually deserted my mother after my brother was born after her separation from my father. Times had changed and new opportunities had opened up so that my mother could find some work to eke out an existence.

With an understanding and co-operative husband, I have been able to try daring ventures that have proved successful. Also, with access to medical help locally, I could restrain my family size. It took me time and a lot of persuading, but I succeeded.

Today we are doing reasonably well and I am proud to say that I have also contributed somewhat towards our success.

If I can educate the children and make them economically independent, I would have achieved my life's ambition. I am not particularly worried about our old age. The children are bound to look after us. The important thing is that they should have enough to share with us.

PANKAJAKSHI

A retired home-maker

Name	PANKAJAKSHI	No. of children lost	
Village	Puthenthura	under five years of age	None
Age	55	Family planning status	Not attempted
Education	Went to school for	Occupation	Prawn peeler
	10 years	Husband's occupation	Tuition to children
Age at marriage	15	Ownership status	Squatter on private land
Dowry	Nil, as it was the second marriage for the husband	Type of house	Thatched hut
No. of pregnancies	Seven		
No. of births in hospital	Two		
No. of births at home	Five		

I have been living in Puthenthura for the last 30 years. I moved here from a nearby fishing hamlet some 20 kilometres away with my husband, when I was around 22 years of age. I am now 55 and my husband, Velu, is 65. We both are from the Araya caste of Hindu fishermen.

We are squatting here in Puthenthura on some two *cents* of private land belonging to a landlord just behind the Government Upper Primary School, very close to the national highway. We chose this area for our hut because of its location. Velu gave private tuition to school children. They came to him for help either before or after school. He charged every student two rupees a month. The village people were always very considerate to us in appreciation of his work. They helped us build and replace this thatched hut. The two benches you see outside our hut were given to us by the villagers for use by Velu's students. For about a year now, Velu has cut down the number of students because of his indifferent health. He feels weak and old. As a result, he makes only 10 to 15 rupees a month. Now that he has so much time to while away, he plays cards with villagers and recites poetry, for which he has a very good memory. Recently he broke his glasses, which was a major set-back. He still continues to use his cracked lens while teaching his students.

The household

We are only four people living in our thatched hut now; this includes our youngest daughter Jalaja, and son, Gyan. Of the two rooms in the hut, each six square feet, Velu and Gyan use one and Jalaja and I use the other. Our room is next to the kitchen, which is of the same size as our other two rooms. We can enter our kitchen only from the verandah.

Gyan, our second son, is now the principal source of our support. Our first son, Dhyan, lives with his wife at her parents' house, as we had some differences. We depend altogether on Gyan's earnings to run the house. He works as a coolie fisherman on a traditional craft. He has been to school for ten years, as Velu was particular that he must have this much education. I thought that with this much schooling he would be able to find a better regular job, but it hasn't worked out that way. Velu still makes a little money giving tuition but that money is just enough to take care of our very personal expenses. Velu can have his tea at the tea shop and buy some beedies to smoke. I like to chew pan and buy a few odds and ends, so at least we do not have to ask our son for these very basic needs. Jalaja has not yet started going out for work. She had such an unhappy experience, having been sent away within one month after we got her married, that Velu and I do not have the heart to push her into anything. Before her marriage she used to go out to peel prawns. On the days she got work she would easily make five rupees a day. Rather than sending her back to work as a peeler, I would like to find another suitable man for her and resettle her.

Jalaja's marriage break-up

Of our seven children, five are girls. Only the first of these girls was married in the traditional way. The next three girls have chosen Latin Christian men and this has upset Velu and me a great deal. Velu is proud of being an Araya by caste. To him, Arayas, though only fishermen now, are the descendants of the Sun god and next only to the Brahmins. We were very anxious that our last daughter, Jalaja, should be married within the caste and in our own village. We both are very fond of her as she is the youngest child in the family and we wanted her to stay close to us. So we arranged the marriage for her to a boy from our neighbourhood. We gave Rs. 500 in cash and a pair of golden ear-rings in dowry. Within a month's time, however, she came back to us. Her husband and his family suspect that she was friendly with a married man. I do not believe what they, or others in the neighbourhood, say against my daughter.

If Jalaja was such a bad girl, they would have found it out before agreeing to the marriage. They belong to the same neighbourhood. Marriage is a sacred thing and it is sad that people take it so lightly and break it on that basis. Anyway we put our case before the village Araya Seva Samithi, our caste association. Since Jalaja's marriage was registered with the Samithi, the boy's party had to return the dowry money. Maybe the Samithi people even put pressure on the boy and his family to take Jalaja back. We had nothing against them. But now, we shall have to look for some other suitable match, but with the blot and so much gossip going around in the village, it will not be easy to find one even if we promise to give a larger dowry.

My other daughters

Our first daughter, who got married in caste, has four sons and two daughters. Her husband owns a *kochuvallom,* the smaller of the two traditional boats found in the

135

village, and her eldest son goes with him on it. My daughter supplements the family earnings by making nets at home with nylon cord supplied by the village dealer. She has now gone in for a sterilisation operation, though late, as a result of great pressure from the hospital authorities. She had all her children at the Indo-Norwegian Medical Centre Hospital (a government hospital). Unfortunately, her last son is mentally retarded. They live in one of the 100 brick houses built by the government for fishermen in this village.

Our second daughter was also married in caste, but some years after her marriage she developed a relationship with a Christian man who was working with her in the same peeling shed in Sakthikulangara. There are no fixed hours of work for these women. When the catch is poor, not all sheds have work to offer. Also, on some days one may get work for just a couple of hours. On the other hand, when the catch is very good, the peeling sheds ask you to work overnight because peeling cannot be put off for the next day. The families have no way of knowing why their girls have not returned home, on account of work or something else. The men, who have become newly rich over the past ten to twenty years because of the enormous increase in the availability of and business in prawns in this area will not stop at anything to acquire what money can get for them. Our second daughter fell prey to the lures of one such man. We have had no contact with her ever since she went away to him.

Our third and fourth daughters are married to Christian boys and are staying in our own village. It came to us as a great shock when our third daughter, Suprabha, announced that she was getting married to the Christian boy in our neighbourhood. When we tried to persuade her against it on the ground that it would go against her next sister, who too was marriageable, because no one in our caste would then accept her, immediately her fiance offered that his brother would marry the younger sister. Thus we were left with no option. Velu has, however, never reconciled himself to this. At the same time, we have not altogether cut ourselves off from these two daughters. After all we did give our consent to their marriage even though it was, more or less, forced down our throats. Of these two girls, the first has two daughters and her husband has undergone vasectomy. The second has three sons and she herself has undergone sterilisation. The children of these two girls were born in the Project hospital.

Our early background

Originally, both Velu and I come from the neighbouring village of Chirayinkil, some eight kilometres away from Puthenthura. People consider Puthenthura as an offshoot of Chirayinkil since most families in these two villages are related to each other. This is particularly true of all the Arayas of the two villages.

My father not only owned a *kochuvallom* and a *valiavallom,* but also had some 12 *cents* of land. We were six children, two boys and four girls. All of us were delivered in the house with the help of the village midwife known locally as Padichi. We all were sent to school, but we stayed in school for varying periods depending on our interest in scholastic pursuits. My brother and two sisters went to school only for three to four years. I went to school for ten years and can read and write fluently.

My marriage to Velu

Velu approached my parents and asked for me in marriage without dowry. His problem was that his first wife, a daughter of his mother's brother, had left him. As his mother had died in a smallpox epidemic leaving behind two rather young children, Velu's family needed someone to look after them. Though Velu's father was reasonably well off, being a dry fish merchant, and Velu himself was considered well read, having stayed in school for ten years, my parents were rather worried on the score that Velu had been married once before and also that his first wife had left him because he had beaten her badly. Velu's story was that his father had forced him to marry his cousin whom he never liked. His mother had warned him against marrying the girl because she had known her. He felt he had to be firm with her when he saw her beating his little sister.

When Velu's marriage broke up, his uncle, the girl's father, forecast that no woman would ever marry him, not a virgin certainly. Velu took it literally as a challenge. When he asked for my hand, I was only 14 years and had not yet attained puberty. My marriage was arranged after I attained puberty, at the age of fifteen.

Our children

In Velu's house, I became the main housekeeper and had to act as a mother to his brothers and sisters. Having heard how Velu beat up his first wife, I was quite scared. I went to my parents' house for my first confinement. I had a lot of trouble with the delivery; then to make things worse, the child, a girl, got sick. My parents took great care of me. They spent a lot of money in nursing me back to health. Velu did not even bother much about us. I was naturally upset and so were my parents. For three years, therefore, I did not go back to Velu. Then when he had an attack of typhoid, I felt he needed my help to nurse him back to health. So I took the initiative to go and see him. Looking at his condition and the state of his house, I decided to move back to his house with the child.

After our second child, a girl again, Velu decided to enlist as a gang labourer for road construction in Assam. His father was old and his business was not fetching much income. On the other hand, responsibilities and the money needed to run the home were increasing. Velu would send me money by money order from Assam but no one ever told me about it. Once when I learnt about it from Velu's letter to me, and asked his family, there was a big quarrel. Velu's brother tried to beat me. So I went back to my parents along with my two children. I returned to Velu's house only after he came back from Assam.

Velu returned to fishing and his dry fish business once he came back. We had five more children, three girls and two boys. I had all of them at home except the last one when my condition was so bad that I went to the Project hospital in Puthenthura and delivered my sixth child under their care. Around this time, Velu's father passed away. A friend of Velu offered to help Velu secure a steady job as a worker in a cotton mill in Quilon city. Though Velu had both the crafts and all the nets, having four daughters and no sons at that time made a big difference to his work. Getting labour was a problem and not economical. So Velu decided that he would take up a steady job.

Until almost ten years after our marriage, Velu's family owned both the traditional crafts known as *thanguvallom* and *kochuvallom*. The big craft carries a crew of 12 to 13 members but it can be used only during the months of August, September and October. The smaller one is a more versatile craft which can be used for 250–270 days in a year, if one had the different nets needed in different seasons. You need a large variety of nets as the size of the mesh is important, because in different seasons the type of fish you can catch varies. Velu's father owned practically all the nets to go with these two crafts. Velu's family made money not only from fishing but also from the dry fish business. Velu's father, his younger brother Bhaskaran and Velu himself were actively involved in all these activities. They kept the crafts and gear in good condition and Velu's father made a good profit from the dry fish business.

Over the years, however the business started deteriorating. Velu's father's health was not good and Velu's brother, who was married, had his family to care for and was no longer available like before. The maintenance of crafts was ignored and they could be used less and less. Velu and his brothers decided ultimately to sell off the crafts and gear and share the proceeds. From this time onwards, Velu started going as a coolie fisherman on other people's crafts. His brother decided to devote himself fully to the dry fish business.

Five years in Quilon

It was in or around 1962, when Velu's father died, that a friend of Velu promised to get him a regular job in a cotton weaving mill in Quilon; he decided to make the move. Velu sold his five *cents* of land in Chirayinkil and found a house in Quilon on a monthly rent of ten rupees near the mill. The job was good. It fetched him Rs. 120 every month, but it lasted only four years. Then there was a lock-out followed by a closure. This threw all of us on the streets. This is when I, and three of my girls, started going to work. Two of them had to stop going to school. We found work in a cashew factory. There are several cashew factories in Quilon as it is the centre for cashew plantations and processing. Our job was to peel the roasted cashew and then do the sorting and grading. It was a hard job and fetched us a meagre wage but it saved us from starvation. Velu started giving tuition to young school children. We stayed in Quilon for one more year before we decided to move to Puthenthura.

Settling down in Puthenthura

We decided to move to Puthenthura for various reasons. It was where our first daughter was living already with her husband and children. It was close to Chirayinkil. Also, quite a few of our other relatives, other than our daughters, also lived there. Then, there were opportunities for work for myself and my daughters in close proximity to Puthenthura thanks to the large increase in prawn catches in the area. Not the least important consideration was that living in a village of our own caste would help our children grow up better. This would also help Velu get more tuition work. In fact, our decision to put up our hut very close to the village school was influenced by the consideration that the boys could come straight to Velu from school for their tuition. Here, we were squatting on private property. The few coconut trees around our hut belong to the landlord who has the right to the coconuts and other waste material from the trees. We are squatting on his land with his permission and he is living in a brick house close to us.

My daily routine as a peeler

When we moved to Puthenthura, plenty of work was available for women in Neendakara, the neighbouring village, only 3–4 kilometres away. My three girls and I started working for the peeling shed of a big exporting firm.

I always got up very early in the morning, much before dawn, and cleaned the front yard and the kitchen. I would wake up my daughters before taking a bath so that they too could start getting ready. After my morning prayers, I would go to the tea shop to bring ready-made tea home for all of us, Velu, myself and the girls, to share. Then there was the morning meal to attend to, because the younger children, two boys and one girl, had to eat before going to school. Also, they would carry some food with them. Around 10:30 in the morning the daily grocery shopping had to be done. My grown-up girls were a great help. They shared all my work with me. They would bring water from the public tap which was just a few yards away from our hut. Also, they would help me in cooking and cleaning. Around 1 o'clock in the afternoon, after our lunch, we would go together with several other women of this village to Neendakara. Different people worked for different peeling sheds. There were nearly 200 to 300 sheds to choose from. It was a three kilometre distance which we would easily commute by walking. On the days when there was too much peeling to be done and it got late, we would be dropped back in the village in one of the company's vans.

The amount of our work depended on the catch. The peak months were the monsoon months of July, August and September. We got work without break in those months. In fact, for many days we would work overtime. Though there were many peeling sheds, quite a few of them were temporary ones that would crop up only in-season. I and my girls were working only for one shed. However, work even in our shed was not regular in other months. On an average we got work for 200–220 days in a year and the payment we received was on a piece-rate basis. The average daily wage worked out to five rupees, taking all working days together.

Work descriptions

The girls and I would go straight to the boat jetty belonging to a commission agent. He owned a piece of land near the jetty and had put up a longish tin shed, 30 feet in length and 15 feet wide, with a proper cement concrete brick house adjacent to it. The shed had an even floor and a drain to the side all around it. The shed and the peeling operations were supervised by the agent's wife and her two sons. The husband had a job with the government at the port office and so he could not run the business. They also had a general supervisor. All boats landing catch on their jetty, if they belonged to Sakthikulangara, paid them Rs. 3 as landing fees. Those that were from the neighbouring districts had to pay Rs. 4 for landing their trawlers. Many trawlers migrate here during high season. This way the shed owner made every day around Rs. 100 just as landing fees. Then would come the auctioning, and the prawns that were bought in the auction either by the lady or her sons were taken by coolies charging

Rs. 1 per basket and dumped on the shed floor. The male supervisor would wash and then ice them. One of the ice factories is close to the jetty itself. During the peak season there is a great shortage of ice. The prawns have to be iced because the trawlers do not carry any ice on their trips. Once the prawns reached the shed, our work started. We usually were there waiting from 1 o'clock for the incoming catch. The shed equipment consisted of just a table and chair and a huge weighing scale. We all would squat on our haunches and peel the prawns. We were paid approximately 15 *paise* to 30 *paise* per kilogram. The excess water would drain away through the drain all around the shed. The shed had many aluminium basins for us to place the peeled meat. Each basin holds around two kilograms.

When there was plenty of work each one of us could peel 50 kilos in a day. Then we got back home only around 10 p.m. If there was no work, we had to go home or go to other sheds. Then the shed would be rented to others for use. The job varied from just cutting the heads and tails, to removing the shells, to deveining them completely depending upon the requirements. The rates for all the different varieties varied per basin from 15 to 21 paise per kilogram a couple of years back. These would then be carried inside the factory for further processing. The methods of processing varied and the shed supervisor, a male, would give us the instructions, though by experience we knew exactly what needed to be done.

If the prawns were of big sizes, meaning about 91–100 to a pound, just the head had to be removed and the remainder washed and iced. Naran, Kandan, and Kara are varieties of large prawns. The other small varieties are beheaded first, then the shells peeled off and the veins removed. We do not have any gadget to do this. Shell particles, vein bits, fibres and other dirt are removed from the meat by continuous washing with clean water. All this meant sitting on our haunches in wet and damp surroundings from 2 p.m. to 8 p.m. and sometimes much later. We were paid according to the basins we had peeled. We could make on a normal day Rs. 7 and on an overtime day Rs. 15. What made the work hard was the highly unhygienic surroundings and the lack of any basic amenities like toilets and drinking water. We were paid on the meat content, so a bigger variety would give a 60 per cent return and a small one which needed to be deveined gave us only 20 to 30 per cent of meat, but the wage rate was slightly higher.

Present position

Since the last two years, I have not been doing any work. Until Dhyan got angry and moved out, the two boys were working and they together ran the house. Now we are completely dependent on our unmarried son Gyan. Velu and I spend our time praying at home, and going to temples and making nylon nets in our spare time. Both Dhyan and Gyan are virtually bonded to two different craft owners. They both have borrowed over the last few years sums adding up to Rs. 500 and can go looking for work elsewhere only after they repay the debt.

We have received Jalaja's dowry money back, but must get her remarried somehow. Until that time it is a great mental strain on us. We will probably have to send her out of the village as there is so much gossip about her here. When Dhyan comes back from his wife's house and stays with us, maybe we can live more happily for some time.

Our future is what worries us more than anything else.

140

CHAPTER V

WOMEN'S CHANGING ROLES

The micro-level information collected through the autobiographies of the women from the study area enables us to supplement the insights gained at the macro level as to how the women have been affected by the various developments spurred by the modernisation of fishing and fish preservation coupled with the discovery of a rich prawn ground for which there existed a ready market in developed countries.

Here we must start by pointing out that the implicit assumption which underlay the modernisation project as originally conceived and designed was that fisherwomen had little, if any, direct active role to play in whatever was supposed to be achieved by way of improvement in fish production and income through technological changes in fishing and fish preservation. This assumption was highly arguable because even though women from fishing households were never directly engaged in what may be narrowly defined as fishing, they always participated in a number of related activities, not all of which were necessarily paid, which supplemented the average household's income-earning capacity. Unfortunately, there is hardly a census or survey that has adequately captured the full extent of work participation by women from the fishing households. This is as true today as it was a generation ago. Still, on the basis of whatever macro-level information we could collect, it appears that women's work participation has increased considerably in the three study villages. The picture that emerges with respect to work participation by women from the fishing households, both as it was some 30 years ago and also as it is today after a major technological change has come about in the villages under study, is discussed in this part.

Involvement in work of the previous generation

The ideal norm both now and in the previous generation among both the Araya Hindu and Latin Catholic fishing households is for women to devote all their time to housework and not to seek work outside the home. Working outside the home is considered to be essentially a male job, whereas housekeeping and child-care are considered to be women's jobs. It was felt that by going out to work, women would expose themselves and come into contact with other men. However, from the autobiographies we find that quite a few women from the study villages were doing something besides their day-to-day housekeeping even in the previous generation in spite of the norm. Women in the Catholic villages reported remembering their mothers husking rice, dealing in broken rice, collecting shells, vending fish, making nets and defibring coir. Among the Arayas, coir defibring appeared to be the single most important occupation of the previous generation. Net making came next. The fact is that most grandmothers and mothers did have some remunerative occupation. Fish vending by headload was an occupation most frequently reported in the Catholic villages whereas midwifery was more common in the Araya village. While Maggie's mother (Sakthikulangara case study A) was a midwife, and Sarla's mother (Puthenthura case study B) defibred coir, Lilly's mother (Sakthikulangara case study D) was a dry fish merchant. Philomena (Sakthikulangara case study B) reported that her mother was a shell collector. Kadalamma's mother (Neendakara case study A) and also Beatrice's mother (Neendakara case study B) were headload fish vendors and Goratti's mother (Sakthikulangara case study E) worked in a freezing plant. Only Pankajakshi's mother (Puthenthura case study C) stayed at home and was reported as occupied only in domestic chores. Perhaps she did repair nets and dry fish for the household, but it is not reported as an income-earning activity. It is probably true that many of these activities were seasonal and brought in meagre additional income for a household but the fact cannot be overlooked that these women were engaged in income-generating activities.

Work involvement of the present generation

When we look at the lives of our principal respondents what do we find? Several of them had started doing work at an early age helping their mothers even before they got married. Some worked independently of their mother, though in related activities. Maggie (Sakthikulangara case study A) worked as a domestic, Mary (Sakthikulangara case study C) spun coir ropes, Philomena (Sakthikulangara case study B) and Beatrice (Neendakara case study B) collected shells. However, it would appear that the Araya women were less involved in work as children since most of them were attending school. Take, for example, the case of Ramani, Sarla and Pankajakshi the three Araya women respondents (Puthenthura case studies A, B and C). All three have five or more years of schooling. On the other hand, Latin Catholic women respondents had practically no schooling and were totally illiterate. This is probably one reason for the Araya women not taking to work as children. Some of the Latin Catholic women gave up work after they got married, while others took work that would bring in slightly higher earnings. For instance, Maggie (Sakthikulangara case study A) became a headload fish vendor soon after her marriage. Now, she is engaged in fish trade as an agent and does not go hawking fish from door to door.

What is noteworthy is that only two out of our ten respondents are not engaged in some income-earning activity now. However, several of them were confined to their houses bearing and rearing children for the first few years after their marriage. It is equally noteworthy that the work they are now engaged in is quite different in nature and income generation from what their mothers were engaged in or what they themselves did as children. Mary (Sakthikulangara case study C) for instance, was herself spinning coir ropes as a child while her mother defibred coir husks. She is now engaged in fish trade as an agent in prawns. Beatrice (Neendakara case study B) also has graduated from shell collection to fish trade while Kadalamma (Neendakara case study A) has been able to switch over from headload fish vending to the management of her household boats. Sarla (Puthenthura case study B) runs a mutual savings club and a woman's tea shop while Ramani (Puthenthura case study A) started making nylon trawl nets for use in the mechanised boats. Pankajakshi (Puthenthura case study C) worked as a peeler of prawns for wages for several years but has lately taken to net making at home. Mary (Sakthikulangara case study C) works as a peeler of prawns for wages, whereas Goratti (Sakthikulangara case study E) runs a peeling shed.

Not only has the type of work changed in each case, but also the income such work yields has improved considerably. Since fishing, mechanised as well as traditional, is still highly seasonal, the associated activities have also tended to be equally seasonal in terms of the employment and income they offer.

For the present generation, particularly those born in the 1950s, work opportunities definitely seem to have increased among both groups, the main difference being that work opportunities within easy reach of women from Catholic villages were far more remunerative than those open to women from the Araya village.

Involvement in work of the younger generation

What is the involvement in work of the younger generation? Four out of our ten respondents have married daughters, daughters-in-law, or both. They number 18 in all. Only four out of these 18 women are working. The rest are staying at home, mostly bearing and rearing children. There is no doubt about the economic pressure under which their mothers/mothers-in-law were forced into work. But it is not certain that once they are free from the responsibilities of bearing and rearing children, they will be satisfied doing just the domestic chores, particularly when economic opportunity knocks at their doors. Also, then they will not have to play the subservient role they now play as mere housewives-cum-mothers.

It is relevant to bear in mind that all these 18 young women have had better levels of education and better access to medical facilities than their mothers. It is very likely that most, if not all, of these women will take steps not to undergo excessive childbearing. To the extent this comes about many of those not working now may decide to take up some work activity or other once their children are sufficiently grown up.

Thus, regardless of whether or not one subscribes to the view that work participation by fisherwomen was rather low when fishing was pursued on traditional lines, the fact remains that women's work participation under changed technological conditions is vastly different and better paid, judged from the inter-generational changes that our case studies reveal.

Work and change in lifestyles

Involvement in work has brought major changes in the lifestyle of several of our respondents. Work now means not only going out of the house, but also meeting, dealing and competing with men other than those from their own households, making independent financial decisions and handling comparatively large sums of money. Those of our respondents who, by dint of their hard work and business acumen have become reasonably successful in their work, carry a lot of weight in these households. Kadalamma, Beatrice (Neendakara case studies A and B), Ramani, Sarla (Puthenthura case studies A and B) and Maggie (Sakthikulangara case study A) contribute significantly to the family income and enjoy within their respective households a status all their own. In fact, no important decisions are taken without consulting them.

143

In such cases, it has also meant a new kind of role for men. Normally, men in the fishing households are not in the habit of helping in any of the so-called female tasks or taking care of the children, even when they are not occupied full-time in their own work activity. Now with women going out for long stretches of time, men have to take on some responsibility for the care of children coming back from school. Also, men in these households generally get more involved than before in the running of the day-to-day affairs of the house.

The kind of freedom and status that our eight working respondents enjoy, the two non-working respondents, Philomena and Lilly (Sakthikulangara case studies B and D), both Latin Catholics, do not have. They continue to play the dependent, subservient role of the traditional home-bound wife. For these women, their contact with the outside world is only through their husbands or the extended family. These women ask no questions and try not to differ whatsoever with their husbands. It ought to be borne in mind, however, that at least part of the reason why these women have not entered the labour force so far is because of their childbearing and relatively young age, being in their mid-30s. Of course, each of them has already six living children and has now been sterilised, but child-rearing might well keep them tied to the house for some more years. But to go out to work for at least one of these two women, Philomena, would involve overcoming the reluctance of her men to let her go out and mix freely with other men. In Lilly's case, her indifferent health may be much more important.

Literacy level

When we look at female literacy, the inter-generational change has been quite pronounced. The mothers of all of our ten respondents were totally illiterate; not even one of the mothers is reported to have had the benefit of attending school. However, in the case of our respondents, the position improves, but not equally for women from the Araya and Latin Catholic households. While all our three Araya women respondents are literate, having attended school for five years or more, four out of seven Latin Catholic respondents are completely illiterate, not having had any schooling whatsoever; the other three have been to school for three years or less and are now unable to read and write. When we come to the children of our respondents, the position is remarkably similar for both the religions in that they have all been sent to school for a sufficient length of time (with the sole exception of Kadalamma's family, Neendakara case study A). In the case of Beatrice (Neendakara case study B), her daughter has passed through school and is going to college now. Thus there can be no doubt that remarkable improvement has been achieved among the Araya and Latin Catholic fisherfolk of the three study villages with respect to literacy level from one generation to the other. It is noteworthy that in this respect, girls are not lagging behind.

Importance of marriage

There appears to be no change with regard to the ideas about universal marriage. Among both Latin Catholics and Araya Hindus, marriage is universal. Most young men, whatever their physical handicap, have been married. Though among the

Catholics one could lead a celibate life as a nun or a priest, we do not come across a single such instance from our case studies. Both groups subscribe to the idea that marriage is universally necessary and that life is incomplete without it.

Age at marriage

In spite of better levels of education and better economic status, the age at marriage has not been pushed up considerably. However, we must remember that the age at marriage was considerably higher than the all-India average for both groups even at the turn of the century. The concept of pre-puberty marriage hardly existed in this part of the world. Between the two religious groups, the Araya age at marriage has shown signs of rising more than that of the Catholics. Judging by the case studies and parish records, the age at marriage has increased by only about one year in a period of 80 years among the Catholics. The age difference between the bride and groom has remained the same, around six to seven years.

Looking at the case studies, we find that the age at marriage was low, around 16 to 17 years, for all the mothers of our respondents. Although even our respondents themselves were married at a relatively young age, it would still be correct to say that they married at a somewhat later age than their mothers. However it is not quite clear that the new generation of girls is marrying later; at least, this does not seem to be so with regard to Latin Catholic girls. All the six married daughters of our Catholic respondents went into wedlock at the age of 18 or below. In fact, their average age at marriage was 16.5. On the other hand, the average age at marriage of the four married daughters of our Araya respondents was 21. Girls from Araya households tend to get married around the age of 20, whereas Latin Catholic girls, it appears, still get married around 17. Beatrice's daughter (Neendakara case study B) who is in college, is an exception, not at all the rule. One possible reason for delayed marriages among the Araya fisherwomen could be that they tend to take work even when unmarried whereas this is much less so among Latin Catholics. On the other hand, there is, as we shall note presently, a phenomenal rise in dowry among the Latin Catholics and this factor is bound to operate as a brake on early marriage because parents have to put together the necessary resources before they can marry off their daughters. Clearly, however, this factor has not had this impact so far.

Arranged marriages

Among both Latin Catholics and Araya Hindus, marriages are arranged by parents and other relatives. Marriages are agreed as between families, the major portion of the responsibility for finding the right groom or bride falling on the relatives. The main considerations that affect the choice of a partner are caste, religious group, possible dowry and economic position; the family background is also investigated.

In both groups, there are certain rules as to who should marry whom. Among Hindus, cross-cousin marriages are preferred but among Catholics this kind of marriage is prohibited and a large number of other relatives are also excluded from marital partnership. As a result, Catholic households keep a good track of their genealogies. Most families are able to trace back three or four generations. In our case studies, with a single exception, it has been possible to construct genealogy tables for all the Catholic fishing households. The church also keeps systematic records of births, deaths and marriages, which can be a source of ready reference. Among the Araya Hindus, on the other hand, both recall and construction of genealogies have been difficult. Divorce and common law type marriages are accepted by them and their is no systematic recording of vital events. In most cases, we could go back no further than two generations. Among Catholic fisherfolk the general preference is to find a match within the village itself, and in 90 per cent of the case histories we could reconstruct that both bride and groom belonged to the same village. Among Araya fisherfolk on the other hand, a lot of marriage alliances seem to take place within a larger geographical area, covering three to four neighbouring fishing villages.

Spread of dowry

Dowry among the Latin Catholics was of very modest proportions and virtually non-existent among the Araya Hindus at the turn of this century. None of the case histories of the Araya women mentions dowries in earlier times. Many Araya grandmothers and mothers were married without any exchange of dowry at all.

Though dowry is not an entirely new concept in these fishing villages, it did not prevail in the way it does today. If we look at the dowry transactions that took place when the mothers of our respondents got married, we find that most of them got married with a dowry comprising of silver trinkets; only occasionally did a cash sum of Rs. 50 or so pass hands. Of course, then the value of the rupee was several times the value today in terms of what goods and services it can buy. It was only Lilly's mother (Sakthikulangara case study D) who was given some land in dowry and Sarla's mother (Puthenthura case study B) who was given a cash amount of Rs. 300, a large amount in those days. But the situation had changed by the time most of our respondents got married. The older of our respondents still got married with virtually little exchange of dowry. Ramani, Pankajakshi (Puthenthura case studies A and C), Kadalamma and Beatrice (Neendakara case studies A and B) got married with no exchange of dowry whatsoever. Even Sarla (Puthenthura case study B), though much younger in age, was not given any dowry despite the fact that her mother had gotten dowry in her marriage. But Sarla's marriage was not an ordinary one, having been entered into despite her father's strong disapproval. Of our respondents who were in their mid-40s, Maggie and Mary (Sakthikulangara case studies A and C) were given a modest dowry in the form of cash but Philomena (Sakthikulangara case study B) was given a pair of golden bangles and promised some land. Two of our younger respondents, Lilly and Goratti (Sakthikulangara case studies D and E) had to be given handsome dowries. While Goratti was given cash of Rs. 3,000 in dowry when she got married in 1969, Lilly, who got married in 1970, was given Rs. 6,000 in cash in addition to gold equivalent in value. Thus, by the late 1960s, dowry had escalated considerably. It is noteworthy, however, that it is among the Latin Catholic fishing households that the escalation in dowry has been significant.

This could be explained by their recent prosperity in the wake of mechanisation of fishing and the discovery of prawns in large quantities.

Dowry in recent years

With the situation in regard to dowry worsening in recent years particularly among the Catholic fishing households, the parents have to put aside very much larger sums than ever before to get their daughters married. Naturally, they expect their sons to bring in equally large dowries. When Maggie's son got married, his wife gave Rs. 10,000 in dowry (Sakthikulangara case study A); Kadalamma's sons were not far behind (Neendakara case study A). Both these women have given handsome dowries to their daughters in marriage. Beatrice (Neendakara case study B) has been somewhat different than most in investing in her daughter's college education; it is not certain however whether she is only putting off the day she will have to shell out a large amount in dowry or whether she can altogether avoid the necessity of giving away a large dowry, assuming that the daughter will, on the strength of her higher education, be able to secure a regular job and thereby supplement the husband's income.

Dowry among the Arayas

In the Araya village, the dowry situation is not as bad as it is among the Latin Catholic fisherfolk. The sums that have to pass hands at the time of marriage are somewhat smaller. But the Araya fisherfolk are, on the whole, not doing as well economically as the Latin Catholic fisherfolk. The important fact is that the dowry is now no less strongly rooted among the Arayas than among the Catholics. Though Pankajakshi (Puthenthura case study C) got a decent dowry for her son's wedding, she could not give much dowry when two of her daughters were ready to be married; that is why they went away with Catholic men, which is something that the Araya community does not approve of. More recently, when she arranged the marriage of her youngest daughter within the community, she had to give away a dowry that added up to a couple of thousand rupees. It is a different thing that still the marriage did not succeed and the girl is back home with her parents.

Composition of the dowry

Dowry usually is given in cash, land and gold in the form of ornaments. Both among the Arayas and Catholics, the dowry is recorded. Catholics report it to the church and it is recorded in the register maintained in the parish church for marriages; the Arayas register their dowries with the Araya Seva Samithi. Cash is usually handed over during the engagement ceremony to the groom's parents. Gold takes the form of jewellery and is worn by the girl, the gold content and purity being discreetly checked, and any discrepancy resulting in the rejection of the girl. Parents seldom risk therefore getting into such trouble. But troubles do arise.

Mobilising the dowry and modes of payment

Whatever the differences in regard to proportions, dowry has come to stay for good in both groups. The responsibility of raising it generally falls on the father (or the brothers) among both the groups. It is easy to imagine the plight of a father with many daughters, for if he cannot find the money himself, he must raise a loan. Owing to lack of resources, marriages often take place on part-payment of the dowry coupled with a promise to pay the rest later on; parents thus buy some time. Thus, in the case of Goratti (Sakthikulangara case study E) her mother's land was acceptable as security, and she did not have to part with the promised cash amount immediately. In Philomena's case (Sakthikulangara case study B) some land was promised, but a quarrel arose when it was not forthcoming. In several cases, the amount is paid at the engagement ceremony for every one to see, but once the wedding is over, it is borrowed back by the girl's parents as a loan. This happened to the dowry which Ramani's (Puthenthura case study A) daughter-in-law brought in marriage. If the dowry transactions are not kept honourably, it leads to endless misunderstandings, which tend to find their expression in verbal exchanges and sarcastic remarks. The situation is further aggravated when the girl goes for her confinement to her mother's house, as is the custom, and is not called back or not allowed to return unless she brings back the promised amount. Even in cases where the girl has brought the full dowry there seem to be endless misunderstandings with regard to its use. The problem arises because the in-laws feel that the dowry should belong to them for they have invested in the son. The girl's parents, on the other hand, give it on the assumption that the dowry is meant for use principally by the girl and her husband. Nevertheless, the true ownership of the dowry is not made explicit. Usually, the boy's parents want to make use of it either to marry off daughters or to clear past debts. But the unwritten rule is that they cannot ask for it; only the boy can. So they have to gain access to the dowry through the son who in turn exercises his authority on the dowry through his power over the bride. In the initial period, since the girl is usually in a rather weak position, she can often be made to agree to anything, as happened to Ramani's daughter-in-law (Puthenthura case study A).

Use of dowry money

We have had many instances where the husband has used the dowry to buy a craft or boat, build a house or buy a passage to the Gulf. Generally, the bridegroom is allowed to dispose of the sum as he likes with little difficulty and misunderstanding on both sides. But it is when the groom's parents try to use the dowry that complications start. The possibilities of manipulation of the dowry by the bridegroom's parents are many and such instances seem to take place frequently. Sometimes, as happened to the dowry brought by Ramani's daughter-in-law, it is direct; in other cases, it is more subtle and is done through the son. But when such instances occur, they seem always to create complications. In the event of the death of the husband or the break-up of the marriage, as does happen sometimes among the Araya fisherfolk, the dowry ought to be returned. Where there is dispute on this score, the church/Samithi has to step in.

Family size

One of the most dramatic changes that seems to have occurred in the study villages in recent years is with respect to the family size. This came out clearly from the macro-picture and is fully confirmed by the case studies. There is, as has been noted above, no change in ideas about the importance of marriage. Not only is marriage universal among both religious groups but the idea that a new bride must produce a child and preferably a male, without undue delay, holds good to this day. She has to prove her fertility and thus assure the continuity of the family line. Among the Arayas a woman who gives birth only to daughters or one who has no children can be cast off. Sarla's mother (Puthenthura case study B) was asked to go back to her parents as the astrologers prophesied only birth of daughters to her. Ramani (Puthenthura case study A) wants her son to send his wife away, because she has not conceived at all.

Among the Catholics, on the other hand, infertility or lack of a male offspring is not enough justification for separation or remarriage. Beatrice (Neendakara case study B) has had daughters only, but the question of divorce or separation for that reason never arose in her case. Only the death of a spouse allows a Catholic to remarry. Lilly's sister got remarried only on her husband's death (Sakthikulangara case study D).

This tremendous concern over childlessness in both groups is reflected in the religious vows women take and in Ayurvedic potions and allopathic treatment resorted to in the hope of making an infertile woman fertile. One has not heard of potions or vows for a woman to be saved from excess fertility.

Given the tremendous concern over fertility and the arrival of male children, it is of no great surprise that all our ten respondents were born in families with a rather large number of children. Three out of our ten respondents, Kadalamma, Beatrice (Neendakara case studies A and B) and Philomena (Sakthikulangara case study B) came from families each having ten children. Five of our respondents came from families each with eight children; of the remaining two who came from families with six children each, their mothers were widowed rather young. Both Maggie and Goratti (Sakthikulangara case studies A and E) lost their fathers when their mothers were rather young and still in their childbearing years.

As for the respondents themselves, five out of ten have had fewer children than their parents; four have had a larger number of children and one had the same number as her parents. However, the average number of children per respondent works out to be a little higher than it does for their parents, 6.7 against 6. So, the shift towards a smaller family cannot be claimed for our respondents. It is still noticeable that the number of children born to the parents of our Araya respondents was distinctly smaller than to the parents of our Latin Catholic respondents, 4.3 and 6.3, and the same situation obtains with respect to the respondents themselves.

It is when we come to the married sons and daughters of our respondents that we notice a distinct tendency towards a decline in the number of children. Maggie (Sakthikulangara case study A), Ramani, Pankajakshi (Puthenthura case studies A and C), and Kadalamma (Neendakara case study A) are the four respondents with grown-up married daughters and sons. The number of these young couples, as has been indicated above, adds up to eighteen, with women ranging from 21 to 37 years. Six out of these eighteen women have already undergone sterilisation. Of these six (four Araya women and two Catholic women), three underwent sterilisation after having had only two children. All of these three women were Araya Hindus. Of the twelve women who are not sterilised, three are above the age of 30 years. One of these has six children, another two, and the remaining one has none. Of the nine non-sterilised

149

women below 30 years of age, only one has four children, three have three children each, two have two children each and two have one child each.

It is reasonably safe to say on the basis of the above that the tendency towards a decline in the number of children prevails among the young Latin Catholic as well as Araya Hindu fisherwomen, though the latter seem to be somewhat ahead of the former. The data available at the macro level supports this conclusion.

Type of care at childbirth

Not only did the mothers of our respondents have large families, but they also delivered all their children at home with little or no qualified medical help. The custom among both religious groups is for the wives to go back to their natal homes, at least for the first few births. Apart from thus shifting the financial burden of the birth to the bride's parents, the practice was meant to give the bride some emotional and psychological support and also time to recuperate by keeping the couple apart in their respective homes. The separation period among the Catholics is just one month, until the child is baptised. Among the Arayas, it is longer. The elder Araya women feel that this led to better spacing of births. Now with the greater availability of medical help in the study area many daughters-in-law do not even go back to their natal homes.

A certain course of Ayurvedic treatment is given to the new mother in both religious groups irrespective of the means of the household. The faith in and awareness of Ayurvedic medicines is uniformly of a high order and well spread. Most women, young and old, recall the care given to them after delivery. There is not much change with regard to the after-delivery care of the new mother over the years. The major difference now is that with the increasing shift of deliveries from home to hospital, the need for immediate after-delivery care of the mother within the house is considerably reduced, particularly because the hospitals invariably provide after-delivery attention.

Thus while in the previous generation, not only did the mothers of our respondents have large families, but they also delivered all their children at home with little or no qualified medical help. However, all of them, whether Latin Catholic or Araya Hindu, were aware of and followed the traditional methods of pre-natal and post-natal health care. While in the previous generation not one mother had made use of hospital facilities, all our ten respondents, without exception, had been to the hospital for at least some of their deliveries. The three older respondents, Kadalamma (Neendakara case study A), and Ramani and Pankajakshi (Puthenthura case studies A and C), who are now in their mid-50s, had their first few children at home and the latter ones in the hospital. The three younger respondents, who are in their early 40s, Maggie, Philomena, and Mary (Sakthikulangara case studies A, B and C) had only one child each delivered at home; the rest of their children were delivered in the hospital. The remaining four respondents had all their children delivered under hospital care.

In the case of the daughters and daughters-in-law, the question of choice between home delivery and hospital delivery does not even crop up as the shift of births to hospital has been total.

There can be no two opinions that in recent years things have changed remarkably. In Puthenthura, the Araya Hindu village, we do not have one case of

150

home delivery since the government-run Foundation hospital opened its maternity ward. In the two Latin Catholic villages also, though the shift toward the hospital has been very substantial, several of our respondents opted for delivery in mission nursing homes even though they charged for their services. Only when they made up their mind to undergo sterilisation, in spite of the known injunctions of the Catholic Church against it, would they go to the public hospital. The mission institutions would not perform this.

Child mortality

Loss of children at an early age used to be frequent in both groups. Elderly Catholic respondents recalled the continuous ringing of church bells usually indicating infant deaths.

It would appear from our case histories that more than half of the mothers of our respondents had experienced the loss of two or more children and this does not take into account abortions and stillbirths, if any. This position seems to have improved considerably in the lives of our respondents. Though Maggie and Philomena (Sakthikulangara case studies A and B) both lost their first-order births, probably because of their young age at marriage and lack of proper care, all their subsequent children survived. Ramani (Puthenthura case study A) lost three children, and Pankajakshi (Puthenthura case study C) one, but we must remember they both belong to a slightly older generation as they are already past their 50s. If we were to look at the younger married women in their mid-30s, Lilly, Goratti (Sakthikulangara case studies D and E) or Sarla (Puthenthura case study B), we find that they have not experienced the loss of any child. The picture improves even more when we take into account the present generation of daughters and daughters-in-law. Of the 18 married daughters and daughters-in-law, only three have reported the loss of children, one each.

The frequency with which women reported the loss of a first child was higher for births that took place before the 1960s than later. Two factors could be involved in bringing about improvement in recent years: one, the somewhat higher age at marriage, and the other, better care at childbirth, particularly because of institutional help. The general pattern that emerges from our case studies is that the relatively high risks of first birth have been greatly reduced. Relatively high mortality rates that were evident for first-order births before the 1960s do not seem to hold true any longer.

Not only did first-order births meet with greater mortality, but many women reported obstetric and gynaecological morbidity due to frequent childbearing. Women who had a large number of births in their childbearing ages between 1920 and 1960 showed a high proportion of obstetric complication. We have noted five cases of women where the uterus has been removed out of a total of ten. All had more than five pregnancies.

Feeding and birth interval

In spite of the increased affluence, there appears to be no change in the feeding pattern of children. Infants are, as a rule, fed on breast milk on demand. Generally,

151

breastfeeding is stopped when the next pregnancy occurs. In most cases, the pregnancy interval seems to be around one year and a half in spite of breastfeeding. We have come across only two cases where there has been a spacing of six to seven years without resort to any spacing devices. It would appear, therefore, that in spite of the practice of breastfeeding, the interval between pregnancies has been, and continues to be, quite short.

In both religious groups, the idea of using contraception for spacing has not taken root. The idea is to quickly have as many children as one wants and then go in for female sterilisations. The acceptance of female sterilisation reflects also a basic preference regarding who, husband or wife, should undergo an operation, once it is agreed that no more children are needed.

Family planning status

Now that the family is reasonably assured that the children they will have will survive and also an alternative in the form of improved technology to limit births is within easy reach, how have our families responded?

In the case of our respondents' mothers, the question of planning the family size never arose as access to modern techniques of family planning were not available during their times. So, all of them had children until they completed their childbearing period or until there was some biological problem.

However, in the case of our respondents, including those who are today in their mid-50s, not only was an awareness created, but also a facility was brought within their very easy reach in the maternity ward of the hospital set up in the study area during the Indo-Norwegian Project (now run by the government). As noted already, all of our respondents, irrespective of their ages, went to a hospital for at least some of their childbirths. Even those who had three or four children at home shifted to the hospital when the facility became available. Furthermore, by now all ten respondents have been operated upon, the five older ones for hysterectomy, and the five relatively younger ones, for tubectomy. It can safely be said that the latter have undergone an operation with a view to limiting their families even though it was done after they already had a quite large family size. Maggie (Sakthikulangara case study A) had surgery after seven children, Mary (Sakthikulangara case study C) after six and Sarla (Puthenthura case study B) after four. Only Goratti (Sakthikulangara case study E), one of our young respondents, opted for sterilisation after three children. All of them told us that they were advised to get sterilised earlier, but it took them and their families time to make up their minds. It is interesting to note that all of them had reservations with respect to the after-effects of sterilisation and now complain about frequent headaches and general weakness.

In the case of the married daughters and daughters-in-law of our respondents, though they all are still in the childbearing age, as many as one-third of them (six out of eighteen) have already undergone sterilisation, half of these, as already stated above, after having had only two children. Of those who are not protected from childbearing, it would appear unlikely that, barring an exception or two, others would go in for large families, though this can be said with greater confidence with respect to the Araya fisherwomen than Latin Catholic fisherwomen.

SOME GENERAL OBSERVATIONS AND SUGGESTIONS

It comes out quite sharply from our evaluation of the development experience of the three study villages of fisherfolk in Kerala that, though women from fishing households were altogether excluded from the core programme aimed at modernising fishing and fish preservation, they still availed themselves considerably of the various opportunities and facilities the new situation created. This was true of not only women from Latin Catholic villages which had accepted the new technology of fishing but also women from the Araya Hindu village.

The case of Araya women is remarkable in that their menfolk had been not totally forthcoming in the acceptance of the programme of mechanisation. These women came forward to take up whatever new opportunities of work were created as a result of the phenomenal growth in economic activity in the wake of mechanisation and discovery of prawn grounds in the area.

Because of access, while women from Catholic villages were able to take up self-employment in trade and processing, women from the Araya village could only enter wage employment either in processing factories or as casual workers at or near the public jetties in the various peeling sheds. The fact that their menfolk were engaged in the fishing trade or related activities was a matter of great support to Catholic women. The Araya women had on the other hand to go it on their own with little support from their menfolk. Several of these Araya women who, for some reason or other, could not go out of their village for work for wage employment, began making nylon nets, a work that fetched some income, however small, and could be combined with housework.

In terms of policy implications, the experience in the three villages clearly demonstrates that there is hardly a development project which does not have a women's dimension to it. Here was a programme for the modernisation of activities which were generally considered as male activities in which women, by tradition, were playing little, if any role. In the design of the principal project also, women were assigned absolutely no role. Still, looking back over the past 30 years or so, it is difficult not to notice the distinct increase in women's involvement in economic activities very closely related to the operations that were sought to be modernised. One is, therefore, strongly led to suggest that as a general rule no development project should overlook the possibilities which the realisation of development would throw open for women on the project's completion. It is not enough to provide, as part of a development project, for the building up of social infrastructure, as for instance was done in the design as well as implementation of the study project.

There can be no doubt whatsoever that if in the design and implementation of the programme care had been taken to assign fisherwomen of the study village a role in the processing, freezing and trading of fish, the participation of women in these activities would not only have been larger than today but also at a different level. Today, their participation in these activities is no doubt very much beyond any expectations they could have entertained, but is still at a level which is either marginal, as in the case of the Catholic women who do small-scale trading and processing of prawns, or very subservient, as is the case with Araya women working for wages in processing factories or engaged in pre-processing activities right at the jetties when the fish catches are landed from mechanised boats. Wages are low and work highly seasonal, and the environment and the conditions in which these women are made to work call for considerable improvement in terms of both general hygiene and the health of the working women.

In net making, where Araya fisherwomen predominate, the relationship is even more exploitative though women engaged in net making have the advantage of working at home. The wage they earn per hour of work from net making is less than half of what a woman earns from work in a prawn processing factory. Net making in the study area shares this aspect of low wage with several other industries in the countries where production is organised on a putting out system under which women from very poor households can be enlisted for work at such subsistence wages. The point of our analysis is that the study project could have been so designed as to provide adequately for such forms of organisation for different types of activities, duly supported by facilities that would have allowed less exploitation.

The battle is, however, not altogether lost in that a number of steps could still be taken to improve matters:

1) provision of training for women in the basics of preservation and processing of marine products;
2) training in the elements of trading and commercial accounting;
3) encouragement to operate in cohesive groups, wherever it is a workable proposition, so that women can undertake to work jointly on a profit-sharing basis and middlemen can be eliminated;
4) construction and maintenance of peeling sheds on scientific lines to be rented out to groups of working women from day to day or even shift to shift in peak season;
5) orientation of deposit-cum-credit policies of various financial institutions to meet the financial needs of these women from the fishing households undertaking activities related to fishing;
6) organisation of net making on a co-operative basis by encouraging and training housewives from fishing households to work together (any scheme or project which proposes to mechanise net making and undertake it on a large scale would be an absolutely disastrous way of tackling the present situation);
7) where women must still work for wage employment, in factories or at home, minimum wage legislation and enforcement machinery to see to it that the legislation is implemented.

While the importance of taking the women's dimension fully into account in all core programmes cannot be over-rated, it goes without saying that all development projects and programmes, regardless of the attention they are able to pay to the women's participation in the core programmes, must always have a strong social infrastructure component. All that it has been possible to achieve in the three study villages in terms of demographic improvements demonstrates in good measure that investment in social infrastructure can yield considerable dividends. We have seen that women from all three villages, regardless of religion, and irrespective of the extent of response to the core programmes, availed themselves fully of the new public health and medical facilities created as part of the study project for the benefit of their villages. As a result, once they gained a greater sense of security with respect to survival of children and as the awareness of both the importance of limiting family size and the availability of sterilisation facilities right at the door step increased, women from our study villages showed a remarkable readiness to take to family planning.

Bibliography

Asari, T. and Menon, D. 1969. *The impact of the Indo-Norwegian Project on the growth and development of Indian fisheries*. Oslo, NORAD.

Bog, P. 1954. *A statistical survey of economic conditions in the Project area*, The Norwegian India Project in Travancore-Cochin, Report No. 2, The Norwegian Foundation for Assistance to Underdeveloped Countries. Oslo, Fabritius and Sonner.

Central Marine Fisheries Institute. 1981. *Marine fisheries information service*, No. 29, July. Cochin, CMFI.

Demographic Research Centre, Bureau of Economics and Statistics. 1977. *A study of sterilised persons in Kerala, 1957-71 and 1971-74*. Trivandrum, Government of Kerala.

Directorate of Economics and Statistics. 1977. *Annual report*. Trivandrum, Government of Kerala.

FAO. 1978. *Population growth and agricultural development: A case study of Kerala*. Rome, FAO.

Galtung, J. 1961. *Notes on technical assistance, with special reference to the Indo-Norwegian Project in Kerala*, Report No. 2-3. Oslo, Institute for Social Research.

George, M.J. 1980a. "Marine prawn fishery of Kerala State", in *Fisherman Quarterly Journal*, Jan-March. Quilon, All Kerala Federation of Mechanised Boat Owners' Association.

George, M.I. 1980b. "Prospects of mechanised fishing in Kerala", in *Fishermen Quarterly Journal*, April-June. Quilon, All Kerala Federation of Mechanised Fishing Boat Owners' Association.

Kerala State, Bureau of Economics and Statistics. 1977. *Statistics for planning*. Trivandrum, Government of Kerala.

Kerala State, Bureau of Economics and Statistics. 1978. *Women in Kerala*. Trivandrum, Government of Kerala.

Kerala State, Department of Fisheries, Ports and Social Welfare. 1980. *Fisheries development and fishermen welfare in Kerala State (1980-83)*. Trivandrum, Government of Kerala; mimeographed.

Kerala State, Development Department. 1976. *Integrated fisheries development project for Kerala*, Needakara Report, Part I. Trivandrum, Government of Kerala.

Kerala State, Planning Board. 1960–80. *Economic review.* Trivandrum, Government of Kerala.

India, Government of. 1951. *District census handbook, Quilon.* Trivandrum, Superintendent of Census Operations, Kerala.

India, Government of. 1961. *District census handbook, Quilon.* Trivandrum, Superintendent of Census Operations, Kerala.

India, Government of. 1971. *Census of India, Series 9, Kerala.* Trivandrum, Director of Census Operations, Kerala.

India, Government of. 1975. *Report of the Committee on the Status of Women.* New Delhi.

India, Government of. 1981. *Census of India,* Paper No. 1, Provisional Population Totals. Delhi, Registrar General and Census Commissioner for India.

India, Registrar General. 1974. *Sample registration bulletin,* Vol. VIII, No. 2. New Delhi, Ministry of Home Affairs.

India, Registrar General. 1980. *Sample registration bulletin,* Vol. XIV, No. 2, December. New Delhi, Ministry of Home Affairs.

Gulati, L. 1980. "Family planning in a semi-rural squatter settlement in Kerala", in *Economic and Political Weekly,* Vol. XV, No. 28, July. Bombay, Sameeksha Trust Publications.

Indo-Norwegian Project. 1964. *A study on the impact of modernisation of fishing on the economy of the fishing folk of the Project area.* Oslo; mimeographed.

Indo-Norwegian Project, Standing Committee. 1960. *A census of fisher folk and fishing implements of the Project area, 1959.* Oslo; mimeographed.

Indo-Norwegian Project, Standing Committee. 1963. *A census of fisher folk and fishing implements of the Project area.* Oslo; mimeographed.

Klausen, A.M. 1968. *Kerala fishermen and the Indo-Norwegian Project.* London, Allen and Unwin.

Krishnan, T.N. 1976. "Demographic transition in Kerala: Facts and factors" in *Economic and Political Weekly,* Special number, August. Bombay, Sameeksha Trust Publications.

Oppong, C. 1980. *A synopsis of seven roles and status of women.* Geneva, ILO; mimeographed World Employment Programme research working paper; restricted.

Pharo, H.O. 1980. *The Indo-Norwegian Fisheries Project and Indian fisheries.* Oslo; mimeographed.